OTHER BOOKS BY MARCIA FORD

Meditations for Misfits
Restless Pilgrim: The Spiritual Journey of Bob Dylan
Checklist for Life for Teens
God's Little Pocket Devotional
God's Little Pocket Devotional for Teens
Shout to the Lord
Charisma Reports: The Brownsville Revival

Memoir of a Misfit

FINDING MY PLACE IN THE FAMILY OF GOD

Marcia Ford

Foreword by Phyllis Tickle

JOSSEY-BASS
A Wiley Imprint
www.josseybass.com

Published by Jossey-Bass
A Wiley Imprint
989 Market Street, San Francisco, CA 94103   www.josseybass.com

Jossey-Bass books and products are available through most bookstores. To contact Jossey-Bass directly, call our Customer Care Department within the United States at (800) 956-7739, outside the United States at (317) 572-3993, or fax (317) 572-4002.

Jossey-Bass also publishes its books in a variety of electronic formats. Some content that appears in print may not be available in electronic books.

Book design by Suzanne Albertson

Library of Congress Cataloging-in-Publication Data

Ford, Marcia.
    Memoir of a misfit : finding my place in the family of God / Marcia Ford,
  foreword by Phyllis Tickle.— 1st ed.
        p.   cm.
    ISBN 0-7879-6399-2, (alk. paper)
    1. Ford, Marcia. 2. Christian biography—United States. I. Tickle, Phyllis. II. Title.
  BR1725.F544 A3 2003
  277.3'082'092—dc21

                                                                2002013075

Printed in the United States of America
FIRST EDITION
HB Printing 10 9 8 7 6 5 4 3 2 1

Foreword

MISFITS ARE A SUBJECT OF CONSIDERABLE INTEREST in my life. Conceivably, that could be interpreted as meaning that I am one of them at heart and that my respect for them is merely a case of like recognizing like. I don't think so, but it is a matter of little importance either way, because the truth is that I would be appreciative of misfits under any set of personal circumstances or affinities. I know this for a fact in every cell of my writer's being. For one thing, without misfits, there would be considerably less for folks like me to write about.

Misfits give texture to life. They also tend, on a routine basis, to challenge the preconceptions that masquerade among us every day as normative behaviors. Some misfits, the ones I treasure knowing personally, do this legally and, as a result, become unwelcome guests at most social events—that, or they turn into self-deprecating wits possessed of an incisive, but nonetheless delicious, line of running commentary... the jesters in life, so to speak. It is this latter category of jester for which I especially thank the Almighty, and it is in this category that Marcia Ford has her place.

Misfittedness as a way of life arguably serves a far more significant purpose than that of giving writers a great deal to write about. That is to say that almost every advancement of lasting merit in human affairs has been the work of an accomplished misfit. By definition, his or her acerbic point of view illuminates with a deadly glare the unattractive and the unproductive absurdities of conformist mentality, thereby forcing the rest of us to abandon it, whether we wish to or no. Despite this redemptive aspect to their work, however, very few misfits ever think of the role of misfit as a particularly attractive or desirable way of being in the world. It is, as Marcia Ford tells us here, far too painful for that because...

...because when all is said and done, when all the jokes have been cracked and all the jesting stories of self-disparagement have been spun, there is still the aloneness. There is still the soul's deep knowing of itself as one without a country. That is what this memoir is about ... about that unrelenting knowing, about the otherness without relief of hearing a different drummer every time the music begins. It is also about a brilliant, clear-eyed, no-nonsense kid who grew up in the early sixties in South Jersey to become a brilliant, clear-eyed, no-nonsense Christian later in life. How that kid managed to remain a total misfit through the whole thing is the warp and weft of this book, thus proving my initial point about the social and cultural (and entertainment) value of misfits. How she found her spiritual home, however, is the tale itself.

Marcia Ford, with all her biting humor and double-edged jests, has given us something more than either quips or stereotypes of Christians. Instead, she has given us the candid, often painful, remarkably humble autobiography of a wandering spirit traveling along all the roads that are American religion, looking—always looking—for a home for misfits. That she finds it, as I too have found it, in the liturgy of ancient Christianity as it has come down to us through the centuries is enough to make me greet her as sister and to welcome this book as the superb apologetic to our communion that it is. That to the very end she keeps her wit as she finds her salvation, however, makes me believe as well that somewhere, somehow, in that glorious beyond to come, I'll look up one day and see Marcia Ford as the jester *du jour* in attendance upon, and on the job before, the throne of God. There could, to my way of thinking, be few better beginnings than that to God's good tomorrow.

Phyllis Tickle
The Farm in Lucy
4th Pentecost 2002

Acknowledgments

IN THE SUMMER OF 2001, A FRIEND and I were driving back to Florida from the annual CBA convention in Atlanta. We were tired, we were wound up, we were overloaded with ideas and information. Uppermost in my mind was this one great idea, prompted by a meeting I had with an author who ministered to exotic dancers. I had edited the book she had written about her ministry, and I couldn't escape the nagging feeling that I should write a book about the relationship between the church and society's misfits. I ran the idea by my friend, Angie Kiesling, as we drove through southern Georgia on I-75. "I have a great idea for a book!" I told her, hoping to counteract the mind-numbing effects of the garish billboards that flanked the highway. "I could write a book on ministering to misfits!" I punctuated my comments with exclamation marks in a vain attempt to keep both of us alert.

Angie, ever the supportive one, summarily dismissed my idea. "No," she said. "You need to write your own story, *Memoir of a Misfit*." That was easy for her to say. She is as much a misfit as I am—most writers and editors are, I've discovered—but I knew full well that she wasn't ready to write her own memoir, so she passed the buck to me. I had to admit, hers was a better idea than mine, but the thought of exposing my life in print was a bit much. It was bad enough I had to live it, and here was someone suggesting I chronicle it. She persisted, and I agreed to think about it, choosing to resume my billboard reading in preference to continuing with this scary conversation.

A week or so later, after some more of Angie's nudging, I ran the idea by another friend, writer and editor Brian Peterson. He loved it. Now I had two people bugging me about it. To shut them up, I came up with a proposal and sent it to several publishers. I was off the hook. No one would buy it, and I could honestly tell Brian and Angie that I had tried.

This is the point at which I should thank Angie and Brian for their encouragement, so I will. I only hope that someday they get to experience the sheer delight of reliving the deepest, darkest moments of their tortured lives. Daily. For a year. With the reading public in mind. Yes, I do wish that on them.

I wouldn't wish the same on Sheryl Fullerton at Jossey-Bass. It's not her fault that I sent the proposal to her. But her enthusiasm for the project transformed my reluctance into eagerness. One conversation with her, and I was good to go. My editor, Julianna Gustafson, not only kept me going during the difficult times but also became a friend in the process. Her sharp editorial eye made this a much better book than it otherwise would have been. My thanks to the entire Jossey-Bass team for getting behind this book.

In typical misfit fashion, I acquired an agent after the project was under way. Chip MacGregor at Alive Communications also lent his enthusiastic support to the book, and I'm convinced he would have been the one to talk me down off the ledge had the going ever gotten that rough.

I am deeply grateful to Phyllis Tickle for the kind words she wrote in the Foreword. A former religion editor for *Publishers Weekly*, Phyllis is a widely recognized authority on religious trends in America. Even better, she is a warm and wonderful woman of faith. It is both a blessing and an honor to know her.

My special thanks to Fay Key and Steve Bullington at the Green Bough House of Prayer in Scott, Georgia, who provided both physical and spiritual shelter for me as I inched toward my deadline. The writing never came as easily as it did during my stay there.

My family gets the lion's share of my gratitude, though I'm sure I'll have to thank them in person because I know they'll never read this page. They have got to be so sick of hearing me talk about this book that I doubt they'll ever crack open a copy. Thank you, John, Elizabeth, and Sarah, for your patience, your tolerance, and every cup of coffee you delivered to my desk.

Finally, I simply must thank every person who ever looked at me funny. Without them, there would be no book.

—M. F.

To John,

*Who is patient and kind, never envious or
boastful or proud or rude; who is not self-seeking
or easily angered; who has never kept a record
of my wrongs; who does not delight in evil but
rejoices with the truth; who always protects,
trusts, hopes, perseveres; who has
never failed me.*

Who, to me, is love.

Memoir of a Misfit

Introduction

PEOPLE LOOK AT ME FUNNY. They always have.

As a child, I blamed my family, that odd, five-member cast of cartoon characters that always walked along the sidewalk in single file so that real families could pass by intact.

As a teenager, I blamed my genes and the local orthodontist. The first had made me skinny and flat-chested, the second had left me with a mouth full of mangled teeth. No wonder people looked at me the way they did; I was a freak of nature and dental technology gone wrong.

As a college student, I blamed fascist, totalitarian America, the oppressive state that had imprisoned me in the dank and dark basement of the middle class, while real families basked in their upper-class glory and bought really cool cars for their kids.

Then I found God. People still looked at me funny, but now I knew why—I was positively glowing with the love of Jesus. How could anyone glimpse the radiance of His love emanating from my very being and not look at me in wide-eyed wonder?

Finally, I thought, *I belong.* I was now a bona fide member of the family of God. At first, like the apostle Paul, I was temporarily—and mercifully—blinded by the dazzling presence of the Lord Himself. As I regained my sight during those first few months of spiritual bliss, the image of my newfound family began to come into focus. Rubbing my eyes, I could hardly wait to see them clearly, to embrace each and every kindred spirit. Finally, there they were, my brothers and sisters in Christ—all looking at me funny.

This is mostly the story of one misfit, and what's worse, a spiritual misfit. But it's also the story of the many misfits I've met along the way. I've encountered some, of course, that would scare the daylights out of you, but that's not the kind of person I'm talking about.

Misfits like me are a bit off kilter but are otherwise productive members of society—a society that cannot figure out what planet we came from.

Misfits tend to find each other. We're the ones that the church doesn't quite know what to do with, and so we huddle together off to the side, wondering how we managed to baffle even those who are supposed to have the mind of Christ. Most of us face the powerful, ongoing temptation to retreat into our already isolated and lonely selves, especially at church. More often than not, we give in to the temptation, back away, and assure ourselves that things will get better. *Someday, we'll fit in.*

In a sense, of course, all believers are strangers in a strange land—some, as they say, are just stranger than others. That would be my friends and me. And if life is this great big puzzle, as still others say it is, then we're the pieces that will drive you crazy as you try to place us in the particular portion of the puzzle you're working on. If you've ever fought with a puzzle piece that just won't go where you think it should, you have an inkling of what you're up against. We won't fit, no matter how long you stare at us, how much you handle us, or how many different ways you turn us around. Push and pound all you want—we're accustomed to abuse—you'll just end up putting us off to the side out of sheer frustration.

Really, we're not being difficult. We're just made different. We're not happy about that, by the way, in case you think we define *different* as "superior." No, most of us have dramatically, even mournfully asked, *Why me, God?* and all we've gotten in response is *Why not you?* We're on our own in sorting all this out, it seems.

I'm not buying that, though. Instead of asking why, I've started asking God to explain a few things to me, like how He can use someone so out of whack to draw people to Christ, what He plans to do about this church problem misfits appear to have, and whether there's any hope for a cure. I don't know if He'll answer those questions, but I do know this—He's been with me throughout my entire life as a misfit, whether I knew it at the time or not, and so He can help me sort it all out as I look back at where I've been.

And I know this as well: Many, many women—and men, too—feel as out of place in society and in the church as I do. We're not alone. We don't need to back away and retreat into our individual selves. We can contribute something worthwhile and valuable to society and the church. And we're in good company: We have each other, and we have Jesus. More than anyone that ever lived, He understands how it feels to be a misfit.

After all, people looked at Him funny, too.

CHAPTER 1

*P*eople who claim to have no regrets are either deluded or full of it. At least that's what I've come to believe. I'm a virtual repository of regret. I have enough to fill several lifetimes, so I figure all those regret-free types must have dumped theirs on me and promptly forgotten about them. But I'm guessing one particular regret in my life is mine and mine alone: that my brief encounters with organized crime were so brief and uneventful.

෨ඏ ෨ඏ ෨ඏ

I'VE NEVER WITNESSED AS MUCH as a minor mob hit, even though I spent two decades of my life in the mob-infested environs of the Jersey Shore. That's ample time to witness a gangland-style killing or two, or at least a backroom exchange of freshly laundered funds. You couldn't go far, especially if you ate out very often, without encountering some mob-connected politico from Edison or Jersey City or Newark who sheltered his questionable gains in a "failing" Irish or Italian eatery somewhere near Asbury Park. I suspect I worked for at least one of those guys, though my boss, as it were, kept such a squeaky-clean operation that the bad guys would confidently stride in with no fear of ambush.

So I ate in the mobsters' restaurants, drank in their watering holes, dated their employees, and what did I get for it? Nothing. Not once, not even one little time did I get to see anything big happen. Over the years, I'd rack my brains, searching for a nugget of information I could pass on to the feds. I didn't witness a single episode that would position me in the hot seat in court. I'm not saying I should have had a front-row seat at a Gotti or Gambino family outing, so to speak. That would have attracted way too much media attention. A small-time elimination would have been fine with me. Anything to draw a quiet contingent of U.S. marshals ever so discreetly to my doorstep, making me an offer I couldn't refuse: Agree to testify, and we'll place you in the federal witness protection program.

For that one shot at a new life, a new identity, a new history, I'd have spilled the beans in a Manhattan minute. I used to fantasize about the covert thrill of relocating to some deliciously vanilla-sounding place like Dubuque or Des Moines or Duluth, where I could teach English or journalism or write under an assumed name. I would have a once-in-a-lifetime chance to become Victoria Wordsworth or Angelica Whitman, because Christina Rossetti, my all-time favorite name, was already taken. The feds, though, would probably christen me Jane Smith or Mary Brown, but they wouldn't hear a word of complaint from me. And I'd work like the devil to fit in to the community, since that would be the point, wouldn't it? I would have to forgo all of my wacky opinions and force myself to look and think and act like a regular person. I mean, my life would depend on it, and even worse, the feds would be looking over my shoulder, at least for a while. It would be my personal experiment in normalcy by coercion.

I've lusted for such a life at various times over the years. I believed that if push came to shove, I could parlay all the social survival skills I've learned into one grand and glorious stab at living like a normal person. So it's a fantasy, I admit, and a complicated one at that. But I wonder if it wouldn't be simpler than trying to make it as a square peg in a round world. Because life as a misfit is far from uncomplicated.

๛ ๛ ๛

IT WAS ONLY AT AN ALTAR OR TWO that I was finally able to establish a new identity. Maybe that's why I got married the first time. I was tired of being Marcia Edwards and everything that name represented—my family's weirdness, my own wildness—so I made a bad choice but got a new name at a time when many of my feminist friends were keeping their family names. But feminism never offered anything remotely as appealing to me as a new identity did. If my second marriage hadn't been so fulfilling, I might have kept on going until I got so far from my birth name that I wouldn't remember it anymore.

Meanwhile, my spiritual identity got even more complicated than my marital status. By the 1990s, I was in my forties and had been Marcia Ford, Christian, for some time. Born-again Christian no less. It had all seemed so simple at one time, but by 1995 or so—well, it was pretty much a mess. I had returned to my once-upon-a-time life maxim: *Question everything*. It didn't help that I was immersed in a faith environment that emphasized joy, joy, and more joy, to the exclusion of other activities like reflection and contemplation. My religious diet consisted of the same spiritual food day in and day out, and I learned soon enough that although spicy salsa may make your taste buds dance in the Spirit, after a while your body starts craving oatmeal. And God, well, He seemed to favor those who jumped the highest and shouted the loudest and swayed the longest. I knew I was not among the favored ones. I don't know, maybe I still had too much Baptist blood running through my charismatic veins. In any event, I started grilling God, questioning Him about what I had done to make Him dislike me so much and why He kept taunting me with biblical promises that were clearly never meant for me. It was time to duke it out.

☙☙ ☙☙ ☙☙

IT'S A SATURDAY MORNING IN MARCH 1996, and I'm in my room at
the Radisson Hotel in Orlando, the drapes drawn tight to keep the
blinding Florida sunshine at bay. Dark is where I am, where I—
almost—want to be. I crouch on the floor in a corner, my back
against the wall in more ways than one. If I can say I feel anything, I
feel spent, but mostly I don't feel much. If you could hook up my
emotions to a hospital monitor, you'd see a flat line across the
screen, stretching off into infinity.

After a fitful night, I've decided to walk out on the love of my life,
the one who has been my companion for twenty-four years. As with
all relationships, this one has seen its share of highs and lows. But
lately, the lows have become unbearable, intolerable, unrelenting.
Our encounter last night killed any remaining shred of desire I
might have had to try to please him. It was over.

This love, the one to whom I had committed my life, my heart,
my everything, was not my husband, however. John was thirty miles
away, dutifully caring for our two daughters so I could be here on
the floor. No, this was not my husband; this was—or is—my God.
He is still God, I think as I sit on the Radisson carpet. He's just not
mine anymore.

He belongs to the other people milling about this hotel, the
place where thousands of women have assembled, all seemingly in
pursuit of God. Well, maybe some used this conference as an excuse
to visit Orlando for a couple of days. A few are probably conference
junkies who figure they can pay someone else to hear God so they
won't have to go to the trouble of learning to hear His voice for
themselves. But let's assume most have come with pure motives,
believing that where two or three thousand are gathered in His
name, He'll show up with a corresponding measure of power. If you
needed recharging, this would be the place to get it.

Me, I'm here because I work for the company hosting the event. I
have a bit part in the proceedings, something of an onstage infomer-

cial for a Christian publication. That's it. I'm here for three days to do my three-minute bit. No one has suggested I do more. No one thinks I'm spiritual enough, I'm guessing. And no one has a clue that because of all this, maybe even because I'm too spiritually expectant for my own good, God and I are about to go our separate ways.

๏๏ ๏๏ ๏๏

THE NIGHT BEFORE MY DRAMATIC departure from God, I had been offered a morsel of hope. The speaker that night was T. D. Jakes. You may know him by name only, and you may wonder why he's such a big deal. Well, this guy had me doubled over with the gut-wrenching weight of the truth he preached. He is an astonishing presence onstage: on this night, a man who has somehow emptied himself of everything that makes him male and replaced it with everything that makes a woman female. It is a stunning achievement. He seems to understand women—their fears, their insecurities, their frustrations—as well as any woman understands herself. This night, he takes the form of an Israelite mother clutching the hands of her children, cowering under the wall of water that rises on each side of her as she leads her babies through the Red Sea, trusting that the hand of God will hold the deluge back until they're safely across. He knows—he *knows*—that every last woman in the auditorium needs to believe that the hand of God is holding back an unseen torrent that threatens to overwhelm her. I stand speechless, numbed by the presence of God, long after he has left the stage. Eventually, I come to and find myself standing next to a co-worker and friend I'll call a nice safe name like Susan. We collapse into each other's arms.

Susan and I had an emotional connection as well as a spiritual one at that time. We had helped each other navigate our way through the depths of despair over the previous year. This night, as we stand in awe of God, several co-workers join us. They've just decided they want to go out somewhere to eat—with Susan. Susan dries her eyes and heads off with them, too dazed by Jakes to realize that I am clearly not invited on their little postrevival jaunt. This clutch of women walks off as one, leaving me alone in the cavernous hall. Well, not quite alone. The stage crew is breaking down the equipment, and the maintenance crew is folding up the metal chairs. I am in their way.

Bewildered by what just happened, I make my way to the shuttle buses lined up outside the convention center, their engines humming as they wait to take the last few busloads back to the hotel. Fighting back the tears, I sink into a window seat, wondering how I could let such a minor incident demolish such an intense spiritual experience. A woman sits next to me, a stranger but friendly looking. She glances at me. I turn to smile at her. She gets up and moves to another seat. Now I'm taking this personally. I do not have bad breath; Certs ensures that. I do not have body odor; Lady Speed Stick guarantees that. I take this as yet another sign that God thinks I am not worth His time or anybody else's.

We drive the two or three miles to the hotel. I get off the shuttle bus and head toward the lobby, veering off at the last minute to take refuge in my car, sitting idly in the parking lot. I'm not planning to go anywhere, although my memory flashes up the name of an isolated road just to the west. For at least the second time in my life, I'm considering the unthinkable. I sit in my car, crying and screaming at God and asking Him why He doesn't just let me die. I'm not doing Him any favors by hanging around; it's not as if He's called on me to do anything significant lately. If all He thinks I'm good for is a three-minute infomercial, well, there are plenty of favored ones who can handle that along with the speaking and teaching and counseling He lets them do. He hasn't had much to do with me for so long that I'm not even sure He wants to hear my voice anymore. I could speed down that isolated road and not hurt anyone but myself. Only

I'd probably end up maiming myself and create an unthinkable burden on my family. I remember my family and realize God's got me locked in to living. I can't leave them, though I sure wish I could leave me.

So the next morning, I sit there on the floor and think this God thing through logically. I figure we made a deal way back when I was born again: I give my heart to Him; He gives me a whole lot of good stuff, like peace and purpose and power. But lately I haven't seen much evidence of all that good stuff that was supposedly coming my way, so I've whittled my hopes down to just one thing—heaven. But if He has promised me heaven but won't let me die, that can mean only one thing: God Himself cannot stomach the thought of spending eternity with me, so He's delaying my arrival at the pearly gates as long as He can.

I figure the ball's in my court now. I play *Let's Make a Deal* with the Almighty. I tell Him I won't bother Him anymore. I'll live a good little Christian life—Lord knows I wouldn't want to do anything to taint His name—but that's it. No more longing for a deeper, more intimate relationship with Him, no more hoping that He'll single me out for personal attention. I may be washed in the blood, but I feel more like a lost soul in the unwashed mass of humanity.

So I basically tell Him, *You go Your way and I'll go mine. Have a great life—or whatever it is that You have—and I'll see You in heaven.*

CHAPTER 2

On Christmas Eve of the kindergarten year of my life, I peered out my bedroom window and spied Santa Claus racing across the clear night sky with his team of reindeer, silhouetted by the brightest, fullest moon South Jersey had ever known.

☙☙☙☙☙

THAT SAME YEAR, I BEGGED my long-suffering mother to take me back to our old house in Atlantic City so we could visit the sweet, elderly woman who worked as our maid, the one who always made ice cubes out of grape juice especially for me.

Neither incident has much bearing on my life as a misfit or on my spiritual journey, as far as I can tell. But each one does reveal a bit about my memory at that time, and maybe even now.

Because, of course, we didn't have a maid. Our family hovered just above the poverty line, carefully clinging to the bottom rung of the middle-class ladder. And although there's no one around to ask now, I think I can reasonably assume that our house in Atlantic City was no better than the place we rented in Arlene Village, a tired cluster of row houses in Millville, New Jersey, circa 1955.

So I'll concede that we never had a maid, though I can still see her rough hands pulling back the handle on an old aluminum ice cube tray that yielded to her determined grip only after it emitted a metallic shriek that made your toes curl. Maybe the maid didn't exist, but she was nevertheless a gentle and wonderful woman, as I recall.

On the Santa Claus incident, I'm not so ready to concede.

I will make one other concession, though: My memory is flawed. When you're a misfit, whether real or perceived, much of what you remember is filtered through the grid of rejection. An incident that seems perfectly normal to someone else is perfectly devastating to you, because you have this backlog of memories that confirms your differentness.

It's in this context that I remember things. And in a spiritual context, mainly what I remember is fear. Not normal, rational fears like the fear that God would strike me dead if I so much as entertained an uncivil thought or that I would burn in the fires of hell if I stopped experimenting and actually started inhaling deeply in a satisfying and intentional way. I had my share of those terrifying moments, but they passed and with them the dread that I felt. My lasting fears were usually much larger and more complex, like the fear that maybe everyone else gets this whole faith thing and I don't. There's a good chance that my brief fling with Buddhism, so brief that all I managed to do was turn its principles on end and walk away with an upside-down understanding of what it was all about, is what causes me to overthink everything, transforming the clearly concrete into the vaguely abstract. Sometimes a hand is just a hand and not a metaphor for some profound yearning in the pit of my being.

This tendency, the tendency to overthink, plagues misfits like me. Because we feel so different, because people look at us as if we're some mild form of freak, we are inclined to think too much. After a while, a simple question like "How are you?" becomes fodder for deep, philosophical analysis, and by the time we've broken our meditative trance, we've forgotten the original question. Now we're convinced that what the person really asked was, "Are you sure you're all right?" prompting the only logical answer, "Of course not." So someone asks how we are, and we tell them "Of course not" and wonder why people think we're so weird.

๛ ๛ ๛

IT'S ALWAYS BEEN FEAR THAT has kept me from God. Fear that I would die of a brain tumor like the little girl the missionary told us about. Why do they love to tell stories like that? I was maybe eleven, and this missionary comes to visit our Sunday school class. She, or maybe it was a he—they were virtually sexless to me at the time—anyway, she was doing fine telling us about why we needed to give our hearts to Jesus and all that. But then she goes and spoils it all by telling us about some little girl who gave her heart to Jesus and a month later they found a brain tumor and the next thing you knew she was dead. Weren't we glad that she gave her heart to Jesus just in the nick of time? Wouldn't it be terrible if we let this wonderful opportunity go by and then we died of a brain tumor and went to hell instead? So, with every eye closed and every head bowed, let's pray, and you go on and raise your hand if you want to ask Jesus into your heart.

Not on your life, lady! I'm thinking. *If I do that, they'll find a brain tumor and I'll die.* I keep my eyes closed and concentrate on this overwhelming sensation of newness, only it has nothing to do with my spirit. It's only the smell of fresh paint in the room we're meeting in. I really wanted to raise my hand this time—I mean, come on, I knew what she was leading up to—but all that stuff about the little girl scared me into running the other way.

Then there was another kind of fear: fear that I'd be left behind. Not by the rapture but by the bus that carried our church group to the Billy Graham crusade in Philly in 1961. Whatever Billy said that day cut straight through to my heart, and right there in the stands, way up in the nosebleed section of Eagles stadium, I gave my heart to Jesus. I was feeling sky high until Billy said that those of us who had just given our hearts to Jesus needed to come down to the field to show the world we were saved. No one in our church group budged. I guess they were all saved already. Well, I wasn't about to go down on that field. I could just see the outright displeasure on everybody's face. *There's one in every crowd. All because of that Edwards girl. Now we're going to have to wait for her and we'll be stuck in traffic and dinner will be late. Knew she was a heathen all along. Didn't I tell you?* I figured they'd decide the Edwards girl wasn't worth waiting for, and they'd leave me stranded there.

As I got older, the fears grew more intense. At twenty-two, a month after I was really and truly and unmistakably saved, I hitch-hiked to Dallas with a friend so we could go to this big Christian event called Explo. On the last day, one of the speakers made this huge deal about making a once-and-for-all, never-let-Him-down commitment to follow Jesus. Well, shoot, I was just one month away from my previous life of sin and debauchery, and although I was on this incredible honeymoon with Jesus, I didn't know if I could hack it for the long run. I mean, I was just too new to all this. I never doubted the validity of my salvation or my desire to please Jesus, but I was so hung up on being good that I was afraid I would let Him down. So the speaker asks those who made that commitment to stand, and about eighty thousand kids stand to make this pledge. The only one not standing was me. Well, there were the kids on the front row in the wheelchairs, but they had a good excuse.

But by far, my charismatic phase had to be the funkiest in terms of fear: Was I really speaking in tongues, or was this some kind of linguistic joke? Did I really fall out in the Spirit, or did I just need a good long rest on the plush carpet beneath my feet? Sometimes, the fear was palpable and wholly external. More than one evange-list has looked at me with such an intense and murderous rage—I was apparently messing up their timing and their performance—that I took a fall just to save my life. Honestly, if you don't fall the absolute first instant that they tap you on the shoulder, some evan-gelists get their noses out of joint and make you feel like a heathen.

And you've got all these bodies on the floor, the near-corpses of the more spiritual, and then the evangelist comes and stares you in the eye, concentrating intently on the Spirit of God maybe but the body count more likely, and you don't feel a thing. So he pushes your shoulder with his powerful fingertips and still nothing. Next thing you know, he's got his other hand pressing down on the top of your head until his palm feels like a too-small skullcap, and still, the Spirit has not slain you. You half expect this man of God to shout, "Come on! Fall, will you?" and by then *your* nose is out of joint and his bodyguards are shooting eye-darts your way and you figure what the heck and send up a quick and silent prayer: *Father, forgive me, for I know not what they do* and you fall backward, hoping the delay hasn't offended your designated catcher. And you lie there thinking, *Well, at least he didn't kill me*—he, of course, being the evangelist and not God, although you can't help but be afraid that your little act of fraud has seriously offended the Creator of the universe. Mind you, this kind of evangelist is the exception and not the rule, if in fact there is any kind of rule among charismatic evangelists. Really, most have been gentle and kind and patient with the likes of me, and some have even been women, but right now we're talking about fear.

I'm still afraid, only now I'm scared that the missionaries will find nothing in my brain and the church will force me to go on the bus with them and the long run will be longer than ever and those pushy evangelists will try to raise me from the dead and I'll be right back where I started from.

CHAPTER 3

I was only nine years old when I first realized I was doomed to spend eternity roasting in the flames of damnation as Satan stood by and licked his menacing chops. Until that moment of discovery, I had loved Second Methodist—Methodists weren't United yet—with all its dark wood and stained-glass windows and two choir stalls. And its fragrance—not of some heathen incense and votive candles, but of earthy wood and mold and mildew. I was too young to know that the mold and mildew part was unintentional. I just figured that's what God smelled like, and I loved it.

၆၄ ၆၄ ၆၄

THEN THERE WAS VACATION BIBLE SCHOOL, a summertime event that took us out of our routines and launched us into two whole weeks of arts and crafts and outdoor games and Bible stories told with the most divinely inspired learning tool of all time, the beloved flannelgraph. You can have all the overhead transparencies and coloring books and workbooks in the world—just leave the flannelgraphs for me. My favorites were the backdrops that showed the Sea of Galilee and the surrounding countryside. Then suddenly, there would be Jesus Himself, with tiny little baskets of bread loaves and tiny little baskets of dead fish! And nothing on Earth could compare with the thrill of being the chosen one, the lucky boy or girl who got the nod to place the Jesus figure on the board that day. Or the Queen Esther figure, on a day when we were using the palace backdrop. It was more than a child my age could possibly take in, much too marvelous and wonderful for kids like us. Those poor adults. Reverend Pedrick must have given them quite a talking to. Why else would they let us—mere children—have the flannelgraphs, leaving them with nothing but books?

Anyway, back in those enlightened days before anyone got the bright idea that kids could be herded off to something called "children's church"—which, as kids today know, often translates into "Worship for Dummies"—before then, we stayed for the entire service, all seventy-five minutes of it—and then trotted off to Sunday school while our parents got to go home to take a nap or fool around or start cooking Sunday dinner. During the adult services, we did everything the grown-ups did, and usually it was pretty boring, except when the ushers took up the collection and you dropped your dime in and got to see all the money and checks other people had given. On days when you were blessed with an extra measure of vigilance, you also got to see who made change from the collection plate, dropping in a dollar bill and quickly lifting out a quarter or two. If no one else seemed to notice, that was even better. That meant you got to share this little secret with God, because you knew darned well that He noticed.

Then there was communion, the neatest of all the neat things that happened at Second Methodist. The excitement of communion always caught me by surprise, no matter how often I partook of the body and the blood. As soon as the usher got to my row, my heart would start to beat faster, and my palms would become soaking wet. Not because of the whole mystery of communion, but because I was scared to death that I would lose my grip on the grape juice tray, and then the sanctuary, not to mention all the fine folks dressed in their Sunday best, would end up splattered with Welch's. Communion was clearly not for the faint of heart. But once I got my little cube of white bread and plastic thimble of grape juice and the plates were safely out of my hands, all I had to worry about was not spilling my own few drops of juice, so I could start to concentrate on other things, like how squishy the bread felt when I squeezed it between my thumb and forefinger, and how much I wished the ushers would come around with seconds because the little cubes and the little thimble were so cute.

෧ නෙ ෧ නෙ ෧ නෙ

WELL, ONE SUNDAY IN 1959, as I sat right there in row seven amid all this breathtaking religious ritual, a bittersweet miracle occurred: I listened to the sermon. I was feeling quite proud of myself until I heard Rev. Pedrick intone the words of Jesus, Matthew 18:3 to be exact: "Unless you come to Me as a little child, you will not enter the kingdom of heaven." The most powerful stun gun on the market today could not have immobilized me as effectively as those words did. The only body parts that were able to move were my racing heart and my reeling mind, spinning wildly out of control with the knowledge that I would not be entering the kingdom of heaven after all. Years of believing I was a shoo-in, what with all the Bible verses I had memorized and prayers I had said and Sunday school lessons I had learned, vanished before my very eyes. Because, as everyone knew, I was not a little child anymore, and as everyone also knew, "coming to Me" meant being baptized, plain and simple. In a gross oversight that consigned me to a reserved seat in hell, my parents, or rather my mother, had failed to have me baptized when I was still a little child.

Before we even stood for the closing hymn, I began trembling. I tried to muster up every ounce of willpower inside me to stop shaking and keep from crying. And there was Merta, my older sister, sitting to my right and looking as calm as could be inside her very own baptized body, throwing ugly looks my way as I fought to find my composure again. Didn't she realize I was condemned to hell? Didn't she care? The only thing she seemed to care about was that I was embarrassing the heck out of her. Of course, she had a mansion awaiting her in heaven, so what did she care? And my mother!

Hadn't she heard what Rev. Pedrick said? How could she so coolly stand up with the rest of the congregation and turn to hymn number 436? Oh, she was a sly one, acting as if she didn't realize what she had done. She must have thought she had fooled me, pretending she hadn't been listening as the words of Jesus echoed through the church, but I could see right through her. I may have been only nine years old, but I was nobody's fool, not even my mother's. I was mature and unbaptized and lost forever, and it was all her fault.

Now that I'd settled the matter of who was to blame for this, I was free to focus once again on the only thing that counted for any-thing—me. I cried myself to sleep for a night or two and then got lost in my fourth-grade world until the following Sunday rolled around. Boy, was I in trouble now! I couldn't not go to church, because I was just a kid and I wasn't allowed to make decisions like that. My insides quivered as I crossed the threshold of the massive church door that morning. I was sure something awful was going to happen, like maybe one of those long pendant lights that Methodists love was going to disengage from the ceiling and come crashing down on my unredeemed head. Kids generally have irrational fears when it comes to things hanging from ceilings, but I had good rea-son to be afraid. I was sitting there in church, looking as righteous as could be, knowing all the while that I was chief among sinners, that despicable type of person I'd heard the pastor speak of with such contempt—a hypocrite. My religious fear was well founded.

Naturally, I couldn't talk to anyone about this, and besides, the verse was so clear. I was far too ashamed to admit to anyone that I had never been baptized, so I just acted as if I had been. If anyone asked—and as I recall, several people did ask—I lied and said I had been baptized. It's not as if my lies made a difference anymore. Once you know you're going to hell, you can lie with impunity. The sins kept piling up—envy that my sister was going to heaven and I wasn't, worry that if my little brother didn't get baptized soon he'd end up in hell with me, and anger that my mother had given no thought whatsoever to my eternal fate. And my father? He was just sort of there, and so far removed from church or anything smacking of religion that I never gave his involvement in this whole ugly incident any thought at all.

೧೦ ೧೦ ೧೦

It's no wonder that I eventually wanted to be an English teacher, because some years later it was an English teacher, and not some learned theologian, who would unknowingly point out the error in my first stab at biblical interpretation. When she casually mentioned that *as* didn't always mean "while," that it could also mean "in the manner of," I wanted to shout "Hallelujah!" right there in class, because now a whole bunch of things made sense, like how the disciples and the thief on the cross could be allowed into heaven. I mean, they were grown men and couldn't have been baptized when they were children. In fact, none of the adults listening to Jesus in Capernaum that day could have been baptized as children, since John the Baptist had been doing his thing in the Jordan for only a few years. So where was the fairness in that? It took an English teacher to convince me, temporarily at least, that God was fair, even though she never uttered His name.

The appeal of language wasn't exactly new, because I had long been an avid reader. I still remember the moment when it clicked, when I knew I could read on my own. I remember the book—*A Thousand and One Arabian Nights*—the way it smelled, the way the glossy pages felt to my fingertips, the magic that lifted right off the page. I must have borrowed that book from the school library a dozen times until I discovered that the same magic was hiding in other books. But then, one simple grammar lesson—and one English teacher, whose name I've long since forgotten—changed my life. I fell in love with the English language the day she taught me about *as*, and this was one love that I would never abandon and that would never abandon me. The adage that "The whole is greater than the sum of its parts" is never truer than when it comes to carefully chosen words. You can take two words and add two more, and if you do it right, the image you get in the end is worth a whole lot more than four separate words should ever add up to. I couldn't have expressed it that way at the time, but all the reading I had done, coupled with this revelation about the multiple meanings of seemingly insignificant words, proved to me that language was worth paying attention to.

But that revelation would come some time in the distant, murky future. I was still in fourth grade, and I was still doomed. My school year would end not with a whimper but with a bang. Or rather, a succession of bangs, one death after another, and in all likelihood, they were all my fault because I had never been baptized and then kept lying about it. Why else would God visit such a disproportionate measure of grief on one little family in such a short period of time? It made sense to me that He was making sure I got a taste of hell. Even so, it was one thing to make me suffer, but He was about to make my whole family suffer. It just didn't seem fair.

CHAPTER 4

*F*airness is a big issue with kids, especially kids in that eight-to-twelve age group that children's book publishers and curriculum developers tend to lump together. Well, I don't know about the statistics and the studies they use to create that age group. All I know is that when I was nine, twelve-year-olds qualified as minigods and minigoddesses. They were adults, practically. And it wasn't fair.

၉၅ ၉၅ ၉၅

THEY EVEN HAD THEIR OWN SCHOOL, for heaven's sake. Seventh and eighth graders got to go to Bacon School, way on the other side of town from the Third Ward where I lived. Somewhere along the line, I found out that *ward* referred to the voting precinct, but it still sounded like a hospital or a prison to me. There was no question in my mind what *third* meant. That referred to our social class. All I had to do was walk the two steps from our front stoop to the sidewalk to figure that out, because from that sidewalk on Green Street, about all you could see were the abandoned mill at the end of our block and the run-down, one-and-a-half story nineteenth-century duplexes built to house the mill's onetime workers. Only I wouldn't have called them duplexes then. *Duplex* sounded so ritzy, like some kind of penthouse. No, these Industrial Age dwellings, with their Yankee, dirt-floor basements, were called double houses. When my mother told people we lived in a "half a double at 410," she was giving both the architectural description and the address. The phrase served to make her point.

So I lived in Millville's Third Ward, where I also attended church, visited the shoe repairman, the kindly Mr. Kolibaba, and bought candy apples from a nice lady who lived across a narrow one-way street from the playground at Wood School, which was brick but named after some Wood person with the initials R. D. Even Arlene Village was in the Third Ward, and so was the tree that used to make my baby brother, Thurman, laugh like crazy whenever we'd stop his carriage beneath it, back when he really was a baby.

It was a shabby neighborhood, but not without character. Just on the one block where we lived, we had a café, sad though it was, and a concrete parking lot for the nonexistent cars of the long-gone mill workers. Even with all the weeds growing between the cracks in the broken concrete, I was able to ride solo on my brand-new ice blue Schwinn for the very first time on that parking lot. I fell only when I looked back and realized my mother—or was it my father?—had let go of the bike.

But the most mysterious element was an incongruous, well-kept "mansion" whose property cut a wide swath right straight through our block, from one street to another. Eerie tales abounded regarding that one piece of property. Surrounded by a high ivy-coated fence, most of the house and all of the grounds were cut off from view. Somebody said an old lady lived there with her deranged adult son, and later, we heard that someone had died there and the body was still in the house. It gave me the creeps to walk by the front of the house, with its terracotta-colored concrete wall and black wrought-iron gate, on my way to see Mr. Kolibaba, who actually lived in the opposite direction. But I liked to live dangerously even at that age, so I took the long way to his shop.

In all our years of living on that block, my sister and I never once saw or heard any signs of life coming from that house. It was the perfect house for the spookiest time in a child's life—made all the more creepy one night by the sudden appearance of a single lit candle in one of its upper-floor windows. I don't recall ever seeing the candle unlit in all our remaining years there.

So that was my life in the Third Ward, and I never expected it to change. But it did, and when it did, my life was uprooted from the inside out.

๑๑ ๑๑ ๑๑

THE CHANGE STARTED WHEN I BEGAN systematically killing off my grandparents, starting with my father's parents. Grandpop Edwards was a miserable old cuss if there ever was one, or at least that's how he exists in my memory. He lived with my grandmother in "half a double at 416," separated from us by two grassy yards, a wide-board fence, and a grumpy disposition that he saved for his family, both nuclear and extended. Down at the neighborhood bar, the one with the tiny windows set high off the ground so none of the neighborhood wives could see in, Grandpop was probably a fairly witty guy, given the dry wit that my father inherited from somewhere. But I cannot recall a single kind word or gesture that Grandpop ever made toward me, even though he always wore this unsettling grin. I doubt we ever made eye contact.

But Grandmom, now there was a saint. First of all, she lived with Grandpop and never once tried to poison him that I know of. Second, she was everything a young girl would want in a grandmother in those days—a plump, kind woman who let us come into her kitchen and watch her make biscuits in the old cast-iron stove that dominated the room. Third, she had the best wallpaper a grandmother could have, almost as neat as the Davy Crockett wallpaper in Thurman's bedroom. Her kitchen walls sported the same scene every eight inches or so, a horse-drawn sleigh approaching a farmhouse in the snow. I'd walk into her kitchen, and my head would start singing "Over the river and through the woods, to Grandmother's house we go." It didn't matter that I only had to walk through a gate and over the cracks in the sidewalk made by the roots of an overgrown tree to get to Grandmother's house.

Finally, she was a saint because she possessed the only icon I had ever seen at that point in my life: a cobalt-blue creamer bearing the likeness and signature of every little girl's patron saint, Shirley Temple. Shirley even had the perfect last name for a saint! No image has ever transfixed me the way the one on that creamer did. I would stand there worshiping my idol in the cupboard for as long as I possibly could. Nothing, not even the objects of my later attempts at Eastern meditation, could hold a candle to the picture of my idol.

Anyway, Grandmom Edwards—who gave me the only birthday gift I remember from my childhood, her presence at one of my parties—got sick with something dreadful called cancer and died in no time at all. Her death shook me like nothing else ever had; when I found out, all I could do was sit in the big dusty-red chair in our living room, sobbing and praying. (Don't even bother asking. Why I thought God would listen to the prayers of someone on her way to hell is beyond me.) My sister rolled her eyes and told me to stop being so dramatic. My mother reprimanded her and said something to the effect that I was old enough to feel genuine grief, and I remember that as the first and maybe only time anyone ever validated my feelings as a child. I'll bet I could have kissed my mother at that moment, but that bit of drama would have proven my sister's point, which I was not about to do.

My parents let me attend the funeral, and was I glad they did! It seems I was the only one there who saw the butterfly lift off from the casket as it was placed in the ground. I followed its flight path and lost sight of it in the pure white rays of the sun, and I knew without a doubt that my grandmother's spirit had left her body at that moment and was already halfway to heaven. So maybe I wasn't much of a theologian, but I know what I saw. I didn't feel the slightest bit of envy that she would be in heaven and I wouldn't, because I believed she deserved to be there. Not like my sister, who was baptized but deserved to go to you-know-where.

Within six weeks or so, Grandpop Edwards must have finally figured out that Grandmom was someone worth coming home to, because now that she was no longer there, he simply gave up and died.

☙☙ ☙☙ ☙☙

So THERE I WAS, TWO GRANDPARENTS down and one to go. My maternal grandmother, Grandma Schwall, had died five years or so before I was born, so she didn't count. But my maternal grandfather was still alive, or so we thought. I had seen him just once, on one of our annual, or maybe biannual, trips to Florida—not the tropical paradise the travel brochures depicted, but those parts of the state to which the Schwalls had dispersed. In this case, we're talking Gainesville, which in the late 1950s was hardly the college football mecca that it is today. Grandpa Schwall seemed to live way out in the country, although now I realize his place was just outside of town. I guess going to see him was such a big deal that it felt like a much longer ride from my Aunt Mabel's house, which was right in town.

His "house," if you can call it that, was a two-room clapboard building on cement blocks in a dirt yard whose landscape was broken only by the sight of an occasional weed. I knew by the looks of the outside that this was not going to be a fun visit with good old Gramps. I followed my mother inside and was immediately overcome by the stench of dried urine and sickness of some sort. All I wanted to do was bolt, but he was my grandfather, and this was the first time I had ever laid eyes on him that I knew of. And what I laid my eyes on was one pitiful sight: an emaciated shell of a human being, lying in a fetal position right on the ticking of an ancient, stained mattress that was just barely supported by rusty metal springs and an iron bed frame. Someone—my mother, or maybe even my grandfather—suggested I sit down, but I wanted nothing to do with this place. Besides, there were few places to sit—maybe a chair in the tiny front room, where his bed was, and one kitchen chair in the other equally tiny room, which contained a small table and what appeared to be an old icebox. Not a refrigerator, but a real live icebox. I hardly maintained what you would call high standards at that time, but this was about the worst place I'd ever seen. We didn't stay long. I don't recall any warmth passing between my mother and her father, and I never asked her about that. I think she tolerated this one last visit because she knew he would die before our next trip to Florida.

And my Grandpa Schwall did die, on the very same day my Grandpop Edwards died, only I don't think we found out about Grandpa Schwall right away. The Schwalls had this fear of long-distance telephone charges, and they'd save money by sending a letter to my mother to let her know when anyone died. That's how we found out that my much older cousin had been killed, "shot right between the eyes" by her drunken husband.

However we found out about Grandpa Schwall's death, I don't recall my mother mourning to any great extent. She had seldom mentioned her father when he was alive, and she seldom mentioned him after he died. She did not travel to Florida for the funeral, which had probably taken place before we even learned of his death.

And that was that. In the space of six weeks or so, through my failure to come to Jesus as a little child, I had managed to cause every last one of my grandparents to die. Now my mission in life was to make sure to add the names of all my cousins and aunts and uncles to the list of those who were never to find out I was unbaptized. They would come after me for sure if they knew I was to blame for wiping out the remnants of an entire generation.

CHAPTER 5

The summer after I killed off my grandparents, the summer of 1960, my mother and father must have thought I needed to get away. Either that or they had figured out that I was the culprit, and they wanted to keep our remaining relatives safe from whatever harm I might inflict. So they packed me off to Camp Malaga, a Methodist campground not too far from where we lived, for a week of fun and godly indoctrination. The camp was right on Delsea Drive, so named because it took motorists from the Delaware River somewhere near Camden all the way to Cape May and the sea, the Atlantic Ocean. Delsea Drive cut right through Millville, so I guess it wasn't too hard for me to get a ride to camp.

ꚛꚛ ꚛꚛ ꚛꚛ

I NEEDED A RIDE BECAUSE NEITHER of my parents drove. It must have been along about this time that I started to get an inkling of just how different our family was. I suddenly realized how ancient my parents were—I had turned ten in June, and my father was already fifty-eight and my mother, forty-seven. Jiminy! They could croak at any time, as old as they were. Plus, they each had been married before, and they each had these other children who didn't live with us and who were so much older than us that they could have been our parents. Well, two of them could have. My mother's other son, Bobby, was only twelve years older than Merta, so he never felt like a parent to us. He just kept confusing us over the years by periodically changing his name, which was actually William Robert DuPriest. First he went from Bobby to Bill, which I suppose sounded more grown-up, and then he briefly went back to Bobby when he met Ginny, but then they both grew up and became Bill and Virginia, which they remain to this day. For the longest time, my sister and I simplified things by calling him Bill-Bob, but never to his face. I loved his last name and wished his father had been my father, until I found out more about his father, that is.

Anyway, my father had two other children, Betty and Margie, and Betty felt like an aunt to us. One of her daughters was even older than Merta, and she felt a whole lot more like a cousin than a niece. Betty and her husband, Jimmy, might have been the ones to drive me to camp that summer, because they carted us around a lot at that time. We'd all pile into their car—Betty and Jimmy and their two daughters, my mom and dad and we three kids—and we'd drive to the shore. I don't think we ever called it the beach, though that was our destination, and I don't think we ever went there without listening to a Phillies game on the car radio. That and the heat always put me to sleep, which now that I think about it may have been the point.

Somehow I got to Camp Malaga one day and settled into the second floor of the girls' dormitory, a wood-frame building that had the uncanny ability to pull every degree of heat from the air outside and bring it inside. We didn't spend a whole lot of time in there. We'd start the day in the cafeteria, go to chapel and Bible classes, and spend our afternoons playing softball. There was even a little store that sold candy and soda, and I thought that was so cool. Snacks for sale, on hallowed ground, no less! The week was going along great until Tuesday night, when one of the kids—I can say with absolute confidence that for once, it was not me—ruined the week by coming down with the measles. So all of us, every last kid in camp, even those of us who had already had the measles and were immune to a second outbreak, had to go home on Wednesday morning. Except, of course, I had no way of getting home.

ᕮᕮ ᕮᕮ ᕮᕮ

OUT OF SHEER DESPERATION, somebody else's mother offered to give me a ride home. I didn't know her or any of the kids in her car, so I just lay low and kept my mouth shut except to give her directions to the half a double at 410. I couldn't wait to get away from all those strangers in the car, so I ran to the door and flew into my house—only to face a room full of strangers. I stood there, paralyzed. Someone asked who I was, and I said I lived there. They all started laughing—there were maybe five or six adults in the room—and this woman told me I didn't live there, that she did. "Oh," one of them suggested, "maybe you're one of the kids in the family that just moved out." "Oh," I said, and looked at the door to see my bewildered driver standing there with my stuff. I choked back the tears and told her my family must have moved and she should probably take me to my father's store.

I cannot imagine today what thoughts must have flitted through her mind at that moment. She probably wasn't the first person to ever look at me funny, but she's the first one I remember. The expression on her face was one of neither pity nor compassion, though there was a hint of both. Mostly, it was one of skepticism—she clearly did not believe that I knew what I was talking about. No parents would move out of a house without telling their children in advance, and they certainly wouldn't do so without leaving a forwarding address. Well, my parents did.

I'm assuming this woman was relieved to discover that I did have a father and he did have a store and he even acknowledged me as his offspring when I appeared at the door. He didn't exactly roll out the red carpet for me, but that was OK. I was out of her car and out of her life, and that was fine by me as well. The only welcome I got from my father was a gruff "What are you doing here?" I told him, and he said we lived in the apartment over the store now but he didn't have time to take me up there, so I'd have to wait on the outside steps in the alley for my mother to get home from work. I did as instructed, and when my mother came through the alley and started up the stairs, I could tell she was just as happy to see me as my father was. She worked in a sewing factory, doing the kind of repetitious piecework that would drive a weaker woman to the madhouse or worse. I'm sure she was hot and sweaty and bone-tired, and I was no sight for her sore eyes.

Our new home was no sight for my sore eyes either. Anyone moving from Green Street would have figured that their next stop would be a step up, but not for us. Dilapidated though it was, 410 had boasted three whole bedrooms, a big kitchen, a living room and a dining room, a bathroom carved out of what had been a pantry, a screened back porch, a full basement, and a big, shady yard that briefly contained a leech-infested outhouse, but my parents had that torn down shortly after we moved in. But now, we were reduced to living in a tiny one-bedroom apartment. That's right—three kids, two adults, and one bedroom. Merta and I got the bedroom. My parents shared the largest room—which in a normal household would have been the living room—with Thurman, who was hardly a baby anymore. He was six years old when we moved in, and only a folding screen between his bed and theirs provided any measure of privacy for my parents. But this lack of privacy may have been the only source of happiness in my mother's life at that time. She had to be madder than a hornet at my father, what with all the promises of the good life up north that he made to lure her away from Florida when they married.

The night I got home from camp, I told our assembled little clan how I had gotten a ride home and had gone to the wrong house and all that, and even my sister felt sorry for me. My father didn't think it was such a big deal, but my mother was mortified. Somehow, adding this embarrassing episode to the rich tradition of embarrassing episodes in our family history was all my fault, or at least that's the way it felt to me. If I hadn't gone to camp the very week of a measles outbreak and if I hadn't directed that woman to what I thought was my house, my mother wouldn't have felt mortified.

Either way, the Malaga measles incident was no doubt the catalyst that prompted my mother, at the age of forty-seven, to apply for a driver's permit. My parents even bought—or in some way acquired—a used car, and I thought we were living large. No more walking to the Laundromat in single file, our dirty clothes piled up in bushel baskets from my father's produce store for all the world to see. No more being forced to listen to Phillies games on the way to the shore, feeling like Betty and Jimmy's poor relations. And no more riding in smelly old buses to Philadelphia for the city's annual New Year's Day bash, the Mummer's Parade, or to New York City for the Easter show at Radio City Music Hall.

᠙᠊᠙ ᠙᠊᠙ ᠙᠊᠙

NAIVE TO THE WAYS OF THE WORLD and the DMV, I was unaware of one minor complication: My mother couldn't drive, or even learn to drive for that matter, without a licensed driver in the car. My father didn't have a license, and we never knew for sure why. For a while, I thought he had once been involved in a fatal accident. When I asked my mother about that, though, she just asked in her most accusatory tone, "Where did you hear that? Now don't you go believing everything you hear! Why, I never!"

So I innocently asked, "So why doesn't he drive?"

"Oh, quit asking me so many questions! You're hanging around me like Grant hung around Richmond!"

My mother, Georgia-bred, had more Southernisms in her verbal repertoire than you could shake a stick at, whatever that means. The meaning of the phrase she had just used—or any phrase that alluded to General Grant—was abundantly clear. It meant "get lost." I did, figuring the story about my father had to be true or she wouldn't have been in such an all-fired rush to get rid of me. I found out later that he simply never quite got the hang of driving.

So my father was out of the running for licensed driver, and Merta, though she thought she was grown up, being a full fifty-one weeks older than I was, was only eleven. Bill-Bob lived in Florida, and we had pretty much used up whatever drive time Betty and Jimmy could give us. Margie, a single parent with maybe six kids—I constantly lost count—wasn't likely to have much free time. So my father turned to his employee roster, which at the time listed one name: Marshall, who I'm sure had a last name but I'm not sure I ever heard it. Since he likely worked for minimum wage, Marshall was glad to make some extra money, and maybe he even enjoyed going along with us to places like Philly, where we would eat at a Horn & Hardart Automat or Tad's Steak House, or to Haddonfield and Cherry Hill, where we bought our back-to-school clothes, or to Atlantic City, where we went to the Ice Capades in the winter—my favorite annual outing—or spent the day at the Steel Pier in the summer. I still have the autograph of some exotic entertainer named Dagmar, her signature being my only surviving souvenir from those summer days on the boardwalk.

Several years earlier, as our little band traipsed toward the board-walk one hot and sunny afternoon, Merta whispered to me that our family looked like something out of *The Toonerville Trolley*, an early twentieth-century comic strip and film series that depicted a motley cast of hapless characters, with names like Aunt Eppie Hogg and the Terrible-Tempered Mr. Bang, hanging out of the windows. The trolley itself was cobbled together with castoffs from even more ancient streetcars, and I had to admit, the image sure did fit the Edwards clan. Whenever we walked anywhere, my father would take the lead, a good four paces ahead of my mother and Thurman, while

Merta and I would bring up the rear. Unless, of course, a family from somewhere other than Toonerville was approaching from the oncoming direction. Then, just like cartoon characters, we'd obediently fall into place, one Edwards behind the other, positioning ourselves in single file so the real-life family could have its well-deserved larger share of the sidewalk.

Only now, we had to try to fit Marshall into the mix. There's no telling what he thought of us or how he figured out our complicated pecking order, if he ever did. What's more, he was black, or rather, "colored"—African Americans didn't exist back then—and this was the early 1960s. My father, being the kind of guy he was, strode on ahead and left the rest of the pack to create our own marching orders. Marshall automatically took his place in back, but that made Merta and me uneasy. Maybe he was just being courteous, but to us it looked like a racial thing, as if he was so used to being last that he thought that's where he belonged even when he was with us. We loved Marshall, and it made us so mad when people would give us nasty looks when they realized that the "colored man" was with us. If the situation hadn't been so infuriating, we probably would have seen the humor in it—that these strangers actually thought this Toonerville family was somehow too good to be hanging around with the likes of Marshall.

My father was not one to provoke confrontation—except with us, of course—so he'd just smile or ignore it when people threw disapproving looks our way. On those rare occasions when a waitress or whoever asked if we were together, even when it was patently obvious that we were, my father would point to Marshall, say, "He's with us—he's the chauffeur," and laugh as if that was the most hilarious thing he'd ever said. Maybe it was. Marshall would grin, and my sister and I would die a thousand deaths.

My mother eventually passed her driving test and became a licensed driver for the first time in her life. We couldn't believe it.

We had wheels, and Mom had a license. I'm not sure who did the most celebrating, but my guess is that it was Marshall.

CHAPTER 6

I didn't know which ward we lived in now that we had moved downtown, but I did know this: Our move had not placed us even a single rung higher on the ecclesiastical ladder. In keeping with our tradition of always attending a church that was within a reasonable walking distance, we left Second Methodist behind in the Third Ward. Suddenly, we had a host of churches to choose from, at least three of which were located within several blocks of our apartment.

୬୭ ୬୭ ୬୭

MY TOP CHOICE WAS FIRST METHODIST, one of those stately looking affairs with a red-brick exterior and pure white columns at the entrance and a spire that reached a lot closer to heaven than the bell tower at Second Methodist did. Plus, it was *First* Methodist, which I figured meant that it was a whole lot better than any other Methodist church in town. The prettiest girl in my class went to that church, along with some of the most nattily attired people in town, so it had to be the best. But we didn't go there.

Across the street from First Methodist was First Presbyterian—another First! Obviously, we were living in a much classier neighborhood now, even if our particular backyard was the parking lot and Dumpster site for the W. T. Grant discount store, where we bought our furniture, and the Model Blouse sewing factory, where my mother worked. First Presbyterian was one of those granite-rock structures that exudes strength and determination, along with a hint of mystery. Now that we lived on High Street, the main commercial street in town, I had the distinct privilege of being allowed to join the Girl Scout troop that met in the church's basement. But we didn't go to services there either.

No, we went to the farthest church within walking distance of our apartment—a Baptist church, Central Baptist. There was no First in that, only central, average, middle-of-the-road. Might as well have called it Ordinary Baptist. Whatever fantasies I might have entertained about our family's rising social status were hopelessly dashed against its mud-colored walls. If Billy Gibson's family hadn't attended that church, I might have turned my back on organized religion a whole lot sooner than I did. With Billy there, I had some-one to keep my eyes on during the service every Sunday and someone to complain about to my diary every Sunday night. Because Billy never returned my loving gaze, or at least that's the best interpretation I can glean from my cryptic diary entries, circa 1961, intentionally kept cryptic to frustrate my snooping big sister. Maybe B. G. really stood for Billy Graham.

Central Baptist. This was the church that invited the missionary in to tell us that we'd better get saved before we all got brain tumors and died the next month. This was also the church that chartered the buses that took us to the Billy Graham crusade, the same buses that kept me from getting completely saved, which I could have done if they had let me because by now I knew all the definitions of the word *as*, and I knew I still had a shot at heaven. Otherwise, I guess the church was OK, except that it was so ordinary. Just don't get me started on the pastor, who had a half-dozen or so kids, and as everyone knew, that meant he had only one thing on his mind. I was finally old enough to know what that "one thing" was. Some people said he might as well be Catholic—may it never be!—with all those kids running around.

꩜ ꩜ ꩜

NOTHING PUT THE FEAR OF GOD in us like the word *Catholic* did. I mean, everybody in the world, except Catholics themselves, knew Catholics weren't Christians. Even the most racist people in town conceded that lots of blacks were Christians, because they had that old-time religion and some of the best gospel songs around. But Catholics? No way. They worshiped the pope and Mary and the saints, and they served real wine at communion, and in their churches they even had *graven images*, an ominous-sounding phrase that struck terror in the heart of my religious being. Surely these people would burn in the flames of hell, which I myself was still trying to figure out how to escape.

Back when we lived in the Third Ward, I would always try to avoid walking anywhere near St. Mary Magdalene Church, because from what I heard, the priests and nuns were so mean that they'd grab you off the street and beat you with a ruler or make you turn into a Catholic once they got their hands on you. There was even a rumor going around that the mansion behind our old house at 410 was really a Catholic convent, and God only knows what went on in there if that was true. Now that I was older, I was sophisticated enough to know that the priests and nuns didn't grab you off the street, but still, I was relieved that I never had any reason to go near their street anymore.

My relief, like so many other adolescent emotions, was short-lived. Now I was in junior high school, and it was time to learn about the way other people lived. In school, that meant learning about places like South America and India. But at the Y, where I was a member of a girls' club, that meant learning about other faiths. Well, not faiths exactly, because we didn't have any Muslim or Buddhist or Hindu members. But we did have Catholics. Somehow, they had sneaked in, and now our club leaders were explaining their latest bright idea: We would visit each other's churches as a group one Sunday a month for the next few months.

Oh, boy! Were they in for it now! The leaders were probably

Catholics themselves, or maybe even heathens, to think of such a thing. The telephone lines in town must have been burning for hours after our meeting that night, with this mother calling that mother to complain about the nerve of those group leaders, who were just barely adults and hardly knew what they were doing anyway, to suggest that their Protestant daughters go to a Catholic service! And vice versa, I suppose! I wouldn't know, because we didn't have a phone in our apartment. If the store phone rang after hours, we'd have to run to lift the trap door leading to the stairs to my father's produce store and hope we'd make it to the phone before the caller hung up. Every time we missed a call, I just knew it had been Billy—Gibson, not Graham—on the other end of the line, calling to apologize for ignoring me in church.

But the store phone didn't ring that Tuesday night, the night our club leaders made the fateful decision to lead us into religious temptation. My mother would not have been included on any kind of grapevine, with or without a phone. She had a Southern accent, and as every Yankee knew, that meant she didn't have good sense and was probably illiterate and served grits at every meal. So the other mothers would not have called her for her opinion on this or any other matter, even if they had remembered that she existed. Which they clearly hadn't.

Our club didn't have all that many members to begin with, and on the Sunday we were supposed to attend the Catholic service, it looked like we didn't have a club at all. The leaders were there, being Catholics or heathens themselves, and maybe one other Protestant girl besides me. And of course, the Catholic girl, or girls, in our club were there; I blocked out their images from my mind almost as soon as the service was over, because I wanted to still be nice to them and I couldn't do that if I kept thinking of them as Catholics. Out of our whole club, there were really only two members there, the other Protestant and me, because we were the only ones whose attendance mattered. After all, we were the ones who had risked life and limb and the wrath of God by daring to cross the threshold of that so-called church, which was named after Mary Magdalene, which says it all.

ᕦᕤ ᕦᕤ ᕦᕤ

CROSSING THAT THRESHOLD OPENED UP a whole new world to me, but it wasn't exactly the kind of world that the nuns and priests, or my Baptist pastor, would have liked to hear about. Because once I got over the creepiness of the icons, the *graven images*, I became acutely aware of the delicious thrill of rebellion growing within me. There I was, inhaling the aroma of the incense, feeling the heat from row upon row of blood-red votive candles, listening to the priest say who knows what in Latin, standing, kneeling, sitting, and best of all, watching the sunlight stream through what I would later identify as clerestory windows, casting a lavender glow over the entire sanctuary. I felt wild and daring and naughty, vaguely remembering that a bunch of Protestants had been burned at the stake because of all this. But they were of little concern to me as I stood and knelt and sat there in that Rome-approved pew. If this was wickedness—and I had no doubt that it was—I was enjoying the experience of it way too much.

So our club visited a different church each month, and I even got to attend a service at *First* Methodist Church. But nothing could compare with the experience of attending my first Catholic Mass at St. Mary Magdalene's. I went back to the services and the youth group meetings at Central Baptist a few more times, although I soon discovered that not even B. G.—either one—could keep me there for very much longer. I was worn down from years of trying to please God with my perfect attendance record. I had tasted the sweet fruit of spiritual rebellion, and at the ripe age of twelve, I turned my back on organized religion. Forever, I thought.

CHAPTER 7

For whatever reason, my mother did not oppose my decision to leave church, or if she did, she voiced her objection in such mild terms that I cannot remember it today. I believe I managed to convince her that ever since the Billy Graham crusade, I'd had a relationship with God that did not depend on the church for its existence. Because I hadn't gone forward at the crusade, I didn't think I was really saved, but at least God and I were on speaking terms again. In my mind, I was rebelling against the church—well, really, against having to go to church—and not the Almighty. Church was boring, but God was not, so I figured He and I could do our thing and be quite happy with each other outside the confines of a church building.

☙☙ ☙☙ ☙☙

BUT I WAS TWELVE. I had no understanding of the church as a living organism, a united body of believers transcending religious denominations and buildings and organizations and institutions. I had no appreciation for the value of corporate worship. And I had no one to walk away with me and hold my hand as I tried to live a life of faith apart from the church.

Not surprisingly, in no time at all, I had forgotten about my earlier resolve to keep praying and reading my Bible and memorizing Scripture verses. Here I was, about to enter high school, and I was ignoring the only sure thing in my life at the time.

The Millville Board of Education was responsible for removing one sure thing in my future when they pulled a fast one on my class, the one that would become the graduating class of 1968. We figured we'd do our time, seventh and eighth grades, at Bacon School and then go on to Millville High School in ninth grade, as every other class before ours had done for decades. But no. Now there was this new idea going around in educational circles that kids should be split into seventh through ninth grades for junior high school and tenth through twelfth grades for senior high school. So the Millville Board of Education up and built a brand new senior high school just in time for the class of '68 to enter ninth grade in the fall of '64. OK, so maybe that did make us top dogs on the junior high school totem pole, but it also meant we had to wait another whole year before we would be in real high school. They did us one favor, at least—they moved us out of Bacon School and into the old high school building, so we did get to enjoy those hallowed halls while the memory of its original use was still fresh.

I'm not sure how my mother knew I was beginning to falter in more than just my faith. Until then, I had liked, if not loved, school. I was the family bookworm, reading whatever I could get my hands on, including a copy of some magazine like *Look* or *Life* that featured an article about the relevance of birth order on a child's perception of herself. According to this article, I was "The Middle Child: Lost in the Shuffle." *Woe is me*, I thought, or words to that effect, and I began to behave in the gloomy, self-pitying way that I thought a child lost in the shuffle should behave. There are some topics, I'm now convinced, that kids should never read about. Birth order is one.

ᕤᕤ ᕤᕤ ᕤᕤ

ANYWAY, I HAD CONSISTENTLY GOTTEN A'S on my report cards and won all the spelling bees and raised my hand in class to answer the teacher's questions. That is, until the day I gave the wrong answer. I was humiliated beyond repair; to this day, I remember the question the teacher asked and the answer I gave—and no, I will not compound the shame by revealing my error here. I remember the look on her face as she corrected me and the lie I told to try to worm my way out of my public disgrace and prove that I was right. But as usual, my face betrayed me, reddening as it always did whenever the spotlight was on me. If I had thought to ask God to change one thing about my physical appearance, it might not have been the obvious things an adolescent girl would ask for, like to have these awful braces removed or to please let my breasts develop a little faster. Instead, I might have asked Him to keep me from blushing at the slightest provocation. I hated it when my face turned red, and I focused on that hatred so much that I would begin to blush all the more readily.

I was still getting A's, so I don't know what tipped my mother off to the problems I was having with school—not *at* school, where things were seemingly OK, but *with* school as a concept, I suppose. Maybe she could see that something had happened that had turned me against school, or maybe she realized that I wasn't reading as much as I used to. Whatever the reason, she took me aside one day and, disregarding the advice of the education experts, she let me in on a secret she had been harboring for several years. It turned out that one of the many achievement tests we'd been given in school was actually an I.Q. test and that I had ended up with the highest I.Q. in the city for my age group. My parents were advised not to tell me, out of concern that I would become either conceited or lazy. As I understand it, the only reason they were even told was so they could steer me toward college prep courses in high school. I'm sure the education authorities in Millville at the time figured that *that* thought would never have entered my parents' minds, and maybe that was a fair assumption.

The education experts were both right and wrong, which I've since realized is an inherent characteristic of all experts. They were right: She shouldn't have told me. But they were wrong: Discovering what my I.Q. was did not make me conceited or lazy. It made me neurotic.

The first indication that my neurosis was manifesting itself physically was a seizure I had at a party, in front of who knows how many of my classmates. The paramedics told my mother I was wrapped around a support pole in my friend's basement. I passed out, came to briefly when the cold night air hit me as the attendants loaded me in an ambulance, and finally came around in the emergency room. The doctors at the hospital could find no organic cause for the seizure; they chalked it up to the combination of heated air and cold sodas. Our family doctor disagreed; he later called me a nervous wreck, or words to that effect. Ever since that night, I've been highly sensitive to flickering light. I have to close my eyes and turn from the window whenever sunlight flickers through the trees as I'm riding in a car. If I'm driving, I have to go through all kinds of maneuvers to block the sun.

And then I began having heart palpitations—again, a chronic condition that began shortly after the party. Next came the chronic headaches, which I figured was my just reward for getting so annoyed at that missionary back at Central Baptist.

But worst of all was—is—the electrical disconnect in my brain. It's like having brain palpitations or the way you might feel if your brain could skip a beat. I'd suddenly realize I was in the middle of a conversation or even a sentence, and I'd have no idea how I came to be in that place at that time with those people having that conversation. It's not at all like memory loss, about which I am becoming quite the expert. I was still just a kid when this whole thing started, so I can't blame drugs or alcohol or old age. It was—is—as if my brain shuts down completely, and then there's a click, and it's back on again. It used to be scary, but like the heart palpitations, I've gotten used to it even if the people around me haven't. Maybe I *am* one of those misfits that could scare the daylights out of you after all.

This I.Q. thing is probably also what started me thinking too much. All that thinking resulted in a million questions, like these: If I'm so smart, how did I get that answer wrong in class that day? Furthermore, if I'm so smart, how come I say and do things that make the other kids laugh at me? If I'm so smart, why do people look at me funny? In short, if I'm so smart, why do I feel so stupid?

For a while, I was dazed by my mother's startling piece of information. But soon enough, I tucked it away with all the other random facts about myself and seldom gave it any more conscious thought. On those rare occasions when my conscious mind gave it entry, I immediately dismissed it, unknowingly relegating it back to a subconscious level where it did even greater damage, chomping away at the foundation of my intellectual and academic life and devouring the appetizing parts of my self-esteem, leaving the bitter leftovers behind.

༄ ༄ ༄

THIS, I CAN ASSURE YOU, was not healthy for a girl just barely in her teens at the time. Nor was the prophecy uttered by one of my relatives, the memory of whom shall not be blighted by identification here. Suffice it to say that it was a very close relative who prophesied that I would end up as an "old maid schoolmarm."

So that was the way it was going to be, was it? I'd show them. I may have been a red-faced, metal-mouthed, flat-chested girl from a decidedly strange family that managed to lose her in the shuffle and at camp, and maybe I wanted to be an English teacher someday, but I was not going to end up an old maid. I set out in hot pursuit of love, not having the slightest idea what that was or what it would look like in a relationship. I'd never seen a living, breathing example of romantic love, let alone marital love, in my whole life, except at the Levoy Theater, where I spent every Saturday afternoon and where the breathing was much heavier than in real life. So, having nothing else to pin love on, I took this romantic notion with me into all my adolescent crushes and practice runs, the stuff of puppy love and all that.

And then, when I wasn't even paying attention, when I was looking in an entirely different direction, love approached me and asked me to dance. In a cruel act of self-fulfilling prophecy, the song was "Go Now." Maybe I should have. Maybe it would have saved both of us unimaginable heartache.

Love's name was Paul. We dated for two years, and today, when adults make light of teenage relationships, I just smile. I have this deep inner knowing that genuine love is possible at such a young age. We loved each other, and we were going to get married. Paul even took me to see the only other guy in the world who could have wooed me away from him, the other Paul in my life, Paul McCartney. Now, that's love. The real Paul, the one who loved me, was two years older than I was, and the day he went off to college was among the saddest days of my life. I grieved for him as if he had left me forever.

Then one night, a guy whose motives were hardly pure hinted that Paul was seeing other girls at the college he attended. Not once in the five months Paul had been gone had that thought even crossed my mind. But that one comment shattered me. I doubt that I ever really believed that Paul had been unfaithful to me — or even could have been unfaithful to me, because faithfulness was so strong an element in his character. But suddenly, I realized Paul was surrounded by college girls — older, prettier, smarter, and a whole lot more normal than I was. By the time I had completed this line of thought, I had convinced myself that Paul would eventually find another girlfriend at college, and besides, he was better off without me. Who did I think I was, inflicting my wrong-side-of-the-tracks self on him? So in the space of one long-distance phone call, I broke off with him, never telling him the real reason why, of course, and in so doing, I pulverized my future.

Not long after, the guy with the less-than-pure motives came in for the kill. I had single-handedly wrecked my life by breaking off with Paul. This other guy recognized the devastation and offered solace. Solace—now there's a quaint euphemism for you. I became a "fallen woman," another euphemism, and to my muddled way of thinking, I had joined the ranks of the biblical harlots, even though I didn't fit the precise definition of one. Perhaps because harlots seemed to be inextricably linked with drunkards in Scripture, I plunged headlong into my two-pronged version of a biblical lifestyle.

CHAPTER 8

For years—decades, really—this one image from that time kept haunting me. One night I was at the Hub, a hangout near the old high school, when a girl named Kathy suggested we walk home together. She lived about six blocks from the Hub, and by then, our family had moved back—you guessed it—to the Third Ward, to the half a double at 416, which had been my grandparents' house before I did them in. Our house was another two or three blocks past Kathy's. So over the years, this fleeting image of that night would surface and then vanish so quickly that I scarcely gave it any thought.

৩৩ ৩৩ ৩৩

THAT IS, UNTIL THE NIGHT I forced it to stop and sit there while I tried to figure out why this particular memory raced across my mind like a streaker at a rock concert. It didn't take long at all. Kathy was cool, Kathy was Catholic, and Kathy apparently didn't mind being seen with me. The kids my age who had gone to St. Mary Magdalene School had been forced to transfer to public schools several years earlier, because there was no Catholic high school in Millville. They pretty much kept to themselves at first, and we public school girls knew why: The Catholic girls had started "doing things" in junior high school. That was the rumor, anyway, and since some of them smoked, well, that was reason enough to believe they might be doing other things as well.

By the time Kathy suggested we walk home that night, we were well into high school, and we had all attended a theologically integrated public school for several years. But still, Kathy's invitation signaled something I never expected from anyone as cool as she was: acceptance. Until that night, I had been somewhat adrift, spending my days in college prep classes with bright kids who lived in brand-new subdivisions with names like Holly Estates—Millville being the "Holly Capital of the World," as we all know—kids who rode the bus because their fathers were executives and managers and they could afford to move to the nicer neighborhoods.

All along, there was Kathy, two blocks away in the Third Ward, and she was fun and wild and crazy, and she didn't think I was whatever we called dorks in those days. So we started hanging out, and I became wild and crazy too. Only—as often happens with adolescents who try to emulate the behavior of others—I hadn't realized that Kathy wasn't all that wild. Crazy, yes. Wild, not really. So there I was, taking leave of my senses, losing control of my better judgment, unleashing the remaining vestiges of restraint, trying to fit in with someone who wasn't all that wild to begin with. She even told me that *I* scared *her* sometimes.

I took to alcohol the way a deer pants after the water brooks. My first taste of alcohol, oddly enough, was such a nothing deal that I don't remember it. I'm guessing I had a sip or two of wine at Paul's house, since wine was a staple in his Italian household. But with two alcoholic grandfathers, I was one of those people who should never have their first taste of alcohol. We never had alcohol of any type in our house, and I never saw my parents take a drink until I was an adult. Even then, it was a rarity, limited to the occasional special event or dinner out.

But during my senior year, I discovered the mind-numbing effects of beer and wine and hard liquor. God knows, I wanted my mind numbed. My life was irreversibly ruined, and alcohol took the edge off the pain. It was also a great excuse for everything else I indulged in; I could just say I was too drunk to remember what I had done. All too often, that was the truth.

And I was still getting A's in school, despite my partying and drinking and late hours, most of which I managed to keep from my parents, who went to bed early. I lived schizophrenically, studying Latin and chemistry by day with my college prep classmates and drinking whatever I could get my hands on by night with Kathy, who grew up around alcohol and never had a problem with it, and our expanding circle of wild and crazy friends. I never knew who I was from one hour to the next; I'd spend an entire class period with one set of friends, the ones who were sober and serious about their future, and then, changing classes, come face-to-face in the hallway with someone I'd made a complete fool of myself with the night before. This was not a healthy way to live.

What's more, I now had to start thinking about college. I know, normal college-bound kids do that a lot earlier than their senior year. Despite my erratic behavior, several teachers told me I had potential and encouraged me not to waste it. They took me under their wing, as much as I would let them. Herr Muenzer, my beloved German and Latin teacher, did his best to steer me toward a good school, though by the time he got to me, his encouragement was too little too late. And if anyone in the high school guidance office knew about this alleged genius in their midst, they never let on. When it came to figuring out what to do about college, I was completely on my own. My parents—my mother with an eighth-grade education, my father with a sixth-grade education—could not help me. My sister had gone to nursing school, so I figured she couldn't help much with choosing a four-year program, and I was too naive to the ways of the academic world to realize I could ask for help from my guidance counselor. What did I know? I thought he was just there to give me a talking to if I ever got in trouble, which I didn't.

One of my friends must have told me about the college catalogs in the guidance office, so that's where my search started and ended. That's also where I fell in love with Middlebury College in

Vermont, my number one choice. It was everything I dreamed of in a school. I would go there and study foreign languages. German and Latin had come easily to me, so my goal was to become more proficient in both those languages and add French and Spanish along the line. What I would do with all this foreign language study was irrelevant; learning for its own sake had not yet become anathema in American culture. I would lie on my bed at night, on sober nights anyway, and imagine crossing the campus with a stack of foreign language texts on my way to the library or the language lab, where I would hole up for hours, if not days, at a time.

I never applied to Middlebury. What was I thinking? Even if I had passed the initial muster and had been accepted, I'd never be *accepted* there. I realized that when I started paying attention to the photos and some of the fine print in the catalog. Middlebury was not for the likes of me. It was for girls from wealthy, patrician families. They would go home on weekends to their centuries-old family estates and enjoy elegant meals served on linen tablecloths, using china plates and crystal goblets and sterling silver flatware. They would even know how to properly hold a knife and fork, which I had yet to learn. And during the week, they'd talk about their daddies and their mothers and their horses. They would wear wool and tweed and maybe even silk. When my thinking reached the point where I didn't know which would be worse, being accepted at Middlebury or being rejected by Middlebury, I gave it up and decided not to apply.

I'm not sure where else I applied. I just know that I was accepted at every school I applied to. In the end, it was the school that offered me a full academic scholarship—Monmouth College in New Jersey—that got the better part of my time and effort for the next four-plus years.

"A third-rate school," Herr Muenzer said, shaking his head sadly when I told him where I would be going. "Well, they gave me a full scholarship," I said, and Herr Muenzer gave me that over-the-rim-of-the-glasses look that I knew so well from class. It translated into, "Oh, come now. Surely you can do better than that." But I couldn't. My parents had no money for college. The state had also granted me a scholarship, this one based on academics and financial need, but it could only be used for tuition and books, not living expenses. I'd have to take out a student loan for that, so a third-rate school with a first-rate offer was the way I had to go. Besides, Ian, my new love interest, attended Monmouth. He said it was a great school, and he wouldn't lie to me even if he did want me on the same campus with him, right? And I wouldn't have based such a life-impacting decision on the advice of my hardly objective boyfriend, would I?

But I still had to get through my senior year in high school and graduation and a summer of working swing shifts at one of Millville's two round-the-clock glass factories.

And I had to get to Paris and back in one piece. In an act uncharacteristic of the Edwards family, my parents had sent my sister on a school trip to Rome the year before, her senior year. How they managed to afford this, even at the ridiculously low student package rate, I never knew. Even though there was no guarantee that this meant they would send me on the school trip to Paris in my senior year, I must have felt I had a fairly good shot at it. Still, the night before the money was due, I cried myself to sleep, only to find a check for the trip on the kitchen table the next morning.

So I went to Paris, where art permeated the very air we breathed—and wine flowed from every vessel imaginable. I quickly figured out how to get to the wine that had been banned by our chaperones, Herr und Frau Muenzer. If I positioned myself at the beginning of the line, I could get into a restaurant or dining room and swipe a bottle of wine off the table before the Muenzers had a chance to tell the *garçons* to remove it. I'd hide the bottle in the folds of my trench coat, and my parents never asked what caused those red streaks that stained its lining.

I also figured out how to get away from the group one night to meet my true Parisian love, Daniel, a waiter in the coffeeshop where he had helped me figure out how to order a cheese sandwich. Only he stood me up, so there I was, unable to meet up with my group without making my entrance really obvious, and nothing to do for three or four hours. The U.S. Army came to my rescue, luring me away from two Germans who were trying to convince me I should accompany them to Pigalle, the red-light district of the city at that time. So these two Americans, one of whom was from Kalamazoo—the name sounded like something comedians had made up—saved me from certain French debauchery, and we rode the Métro for hours, getting off at different stops just long enough to go up to the street and check out the different neighborhoods. I loved it. That night sealed one absolutely certain fact of my future: I would return to Paris someday. Which, as my children today will tell you, sealed one absolutely certain fact of my real life: I would never return to Paris.

CHAPTER 9

*I*t's taken me a lifetime to figure out that the best way for me to guarantee that I'll get to do the things I want to do is to pledge that I'll never do them. Like returning to Paris. Instead of resolving to return, I should have vowed that the one certain thing in my life is that I would never even want to go back. I probably would have been strolling along the Seine within another year or so.

☙☙ ☙☙ ☙☙

THE REVERSE HAS ALSO BEEN TRUE in my life. Virtually everything I said I could never do, I've done. And I'm not talking about the good stuff, like I could never write a best-seller. I mean the bad stuff, like I would never get a divorce. Or some of the other things I did in the late 1960s, well before the notion of marriage and divorce became a reality for me.

So one of these days, I'll stop asserting those absolutely certain facts about the way my life will go. But back in 1968, I hadn't even begun to learn that lesson, let alone apply it. Not only did I never return to Paris, I never even learned to type. That, though, was intentional, because I knew, with rock-solid certainty, that I would never work in an office. No, I would live the life of an academic nomad, never settling in one place for too long. And somehow I'd manage to do that and be a college professor and write papers and books and monographs and all those things that professors must write, without ever having to learn to type or work in an office. I no doubt believed that by the time I graduated from college, the flower children out in San Francisco would have changed American culture so dramatically that meadows would replace offices and calligraphy would replace typewriters.

I really must remember to thank God that I was born when I was, because the hippie movement came to South Jersey at just the right time to provide the perfect cover for my depravity. Now I could say I was expanding my mind and engaging in free love, and that sounded so much better than the truth.

Then too, the counterculture offered an outlet for some of my most deeply held but unpopular opinions. Finally, I had found a group of soul mates who eschewed the American dream of a house in the suburbs and a wood-paneled Suburban station wagon and 2.5 neatly dressed and scrubbed children, looking for all the world like little Tupperware containers. I didn't care how much money I made, as long as my work was meaningful. My Millville friends could go live in Holly Estates; I wanted a simple cabin in the woods or a farmhouse in the country, with only enough electrical power to fire up a record player so I could listen to Leonard Cohen or John Coltrane once in a while. I would never own a television. Friends would stop by and stay for hours or days or years, and we'd discuss the deeper issues of life well into the night, every night. The only evidence of a consumer mentality in my life would be a vast library of classics and literary works and an occasional contemporary release by someone like Solzhenitsyn, whose books I would read in Russian, of course.

Naturally, I did not completely fit in with the counterculture, though I've never found another group that was a better fit for me. Philosophically, it was a perfect match, but politically, we parted ways on several fronts. Of course, I was opposed to the Vietnam "conflict"—another euphemism from that time. But all the talk of peace and love sounded hollow and superficial to me. The most prominent leaders of the antiwar movement seemed to have a fairly good grasp of what we were up against, but what I witnessed on most campuses, including my own, was little more than an exercise in wishful thinking. I don't know, maybe all the things I'd been taught in Sunday school about the sinfulness of humanity played a much bigger role in my attitude toward antiwar protests than I realized at the time. We were never going to change the hearts of people who lusted after power and wealth, at least not on a national or international scale.

Furthermore, my distrust of the government ran so deep that I could not believe that we would get away with our protests without losing our lives at some point. I wasn't afraid to die—in fact, I welcomed the thought of death—but I would not allow the government the pleasure of taking credit for my slaughter. So I lived recklessly in every regard except when it came to the government. I considered the possibility that I was a classic paranoid, but when the Ohio National Guard killed several students at Kent State, I was cured of that self-diagnosis. My prophecy was dead-on.

ଗଏ ଗଏ ଗଏ

BUT THE FULFILLMENT OF THAT PROPHECY was several years away. In the fall of 1968, I trotted off to Monmouth, where I majored in English because I didn't know what else to do. In my most lucid moments, I had a plan, vague though it was. I'd teach high school for a while, earn my master's, teach at a community college, earn my Ph.D., and become a full professor at a university. My lucid moments must have been few and far between, because I did precious little to accomplish those goals. For the first time in my life, I actually had to study. This interfered with my immediate goal, which was to be higher than a kite as often as humanly possible.

Fitting in to the student body at Monmouth was another challenge. Part of the problem, I'm sure, was the typical difficulty that most kids face when they're away from home for the first time. But Monmouth was a relatively expensive school at the time, and here I was, smack-dab in the middle of wealth once again. This wasn't the silk-and-tweed set I would have faced at Middlebury, though; these kids represented the third or fourth generation of immigrant families that had made a killing through hard work in retail sales or whole- sale distribution or any one of countless other industries in the met- ropolitan New York area. Their parents and grandparents had earned their money through the sweat of their brow, and they were going to see to it that their kids never had to do the same. I was sur- rounded by Rosenblums and Marzullos who seemed to have more money than God—who, by the way, had stopped speaking to me once again.

In fact, that was the year God let me know in no uncertain terms that He was finished with me for good. But before He showed His hand, I had a supernatural experience through which I believed God was calling me back to Himself. This was not a conscious thought or a feeling or an idea or even a deep knowing.

I had just crossed the campus on my way back to my room from another dorm when I had an experience I can describe, a flashback to a time of innocence earlier in my teenage years. I was straight and sober the night this image of a purer me dashed across my mind, and yet I could barely recognize the girl that I saw. Had I traveled so far from my true self that I was unrecognizable even to me?

As I tried to make sense of that disturbing moment, I felt the unmistakable presence of God. Alone in my dorm room, with only the haunting memories of my faith as a child, I sensed a supernatu- ral pull toward Him. I felt as if He was reaching deep inside of me and drawing out my dormant spirit so He could restore it. He was beckoning me to return to Him, and inherent in the experience was the assurance that He would restore the purity that I had sensed in the image of the old me. I somehow knew better than to question how He thought He could handle that. In fact, I knew better than to question anything about the experience. It was more real than the reality I was living in. Instead of dwelling on it, I simply accepted it.

I've never been one to sit around and wait for things to happen, which most of the time is a good thing. In this case, it apparently was not such a good thing at all. I set out to determine what I could do to bring about this transformation of my wicked ways. Not once did it occur to me to go to a church, seek the advice of a pastor, or even try to find anyone at Monmouth who might have believed in God. I decided instead to take advantage of a break in the school year to travel a thousand miles or so to visit an older guy I had known just about forever, a man I was sure would help me come to terms with the freedom that up until then I had only abused. I anticipated having long talks with him, in which he would impart to me the wisdom he had gleaned over the years. He would say the right words, and I would see the light. End of fallen woman.

I never doubted the wisdom of this plan or God's seal of approval on it. So inextricably was God linked to this plan that when this trusted older man tried to lure me into bed with him, I took his seduction as a distinct sign that God considered me to be beyond hope. If *this* man could see me only as a sex object, there was little point in expecting other men to see a different me. Ever the guilty party, I assumed I had done something to give him the impression that I would welcome his advances. If that was the case, then I had blown my last opportunity at straightening out my life.

I never even had a chance to tell this man the real reason why I had come to see him. I managed to get out of the situation without any physical harm being done, but the emotional and spiritual damage was incalculable. I was certain that if I could have seen an image of God at that time, I would have seen Him literally turn His back to me.

I returned to Monmouth and to the sordid life I figured I was destined to live. Somehow I survived my freshman year, but my sophomore year was another matter altogether. I had moved off campus into an apartment with several friends, and I made life miserable for them and for myself. I was coming and going at all hours with all kinds of people; my roommates were being pulled into the whirl-wind of my own personal maelstrom and understandably didn't take too kindly to strangers in the house all the time. Before the first semester ended, they made it clear that I was not welcome there, and I could not blame them.

By the middle of the school year, I lost it. I was scared to death that I might really be going crazy. I couldn't seem to keep my thoughts straight, even when I was straight. Often when I was taking a test, I would stop writing in the middle of a sentence without a clue about what I was trying to say. I would have to slowly reread the question, one syllable at a time, to try to reconstruct the answer that only a minute or two before had come so easily. On far too many occasions, I would leave my dorm with a clear destination in mind, only to reach the street and wonder where I was heading. The cir-cuitry in my brain was disconnecting more often than usual, and when it reconnected I'd find myself sitting in class with no idea which class I was in or how I had gotten there. And yet I was still get-ting good grades. It was maddening; I almost wished for some kind of punishment that would bring me to my senses and force me to straighten out my life. When nothing dreadful happened, I took matters into my own hands once again, took a semester off, and moved back home.

That did little good in the long run. In the short run, it got me away from my usual contacts. I enrolled in a few classes at a com-munity college and quickly found a whole new set of contacts. In fact, my new friends had access to an entirely different category of controlled dangerous substances. But they were good people, the best—the kind of friends I could bare my soul to without fear of rejection or ridicule. We would talk for hours about the nature of reality and the meaning of life, speculating on things like how our individual spirits could merge to make us one person and whether that could happen in this life or only in the next. Come hell or high water, we were going to figure out what life was about before it passed us by, even if we had no idea what we were talking about.

Among the group was a guy, his name long since forgotten, who astonished me one night by casually mentioning that he was going to switch his major to journalism and try to get a job as a reporter at the *Hartford Courant* in Connecticut after he graduated. Here was a guy who knew what he wanted to do, knew where he wanted to do it, and had the guts to actually talk about getting a job. This was virtually unheard of in any group of friends I'd had in recent years. We did not talk about anything as mundane as the actual job we might have someday; the closest we ever came to that was talking about our chosen field or profession, never about a job. That was so *bourgeois*, our word of choice at the time. This guy, though, came right out and said the word *job*, and I was impressed by his courage. And the job he aspired to—that of a reporter—sounded so exotic, even in those pre-Watergate days, that I backed away from him, as if I was afraid of catching whatever he had, regardless of how appealing it sounded. I must not have moved far enough away, because once the journalism bug bit me, I was forever infected.

Along with our late-night rap sessions, as our heavy-duty conversations were called in 1970, we attended every rock festival and concert within a reasonable radius. The summer before, I had purposely sat out Woodstock—I had a ride and a bunch of friends to go with, but once I got wind of how big it was going to be, I backed out. I was never comfortable in large crowds to begin with, but this was different. This was a large crowd of my own kind, and that meant free-flowing debauchery, the very thing I was trying to avoid. Plus, in my deeply philosophical frame of mind at the time, the whole thing seemed so—how does one say?—oh, shallow. Yes, I was getting uppity in a low-life sort of way. But mainly, I avoided

Woodstock because I envisioned swarms of federal troops gunning down every last hippie, and I'd rather sit home and die of boredom than let them kill me. I never regretted that decision, and I felt vindicated when I found out that Bob Dylan was just as uppity about Woodstock as I was.

My increasing disillusionment with the whole drug culture became evident at a rock concert—possibly a Jethro Tull event, possibly at the Spectrum in Philly, possibly in 1970. Who could tell now? What I remember most about that night was folksinger Richie Havens. As usual, I had entered the building under an assortment of influences, but by the time Richie took the stage—this was one of those cast-of-thousands concerts—I was good and ready for another dose of whatever pharmaceutical I could get my hands on. But I got my hands on nothing, and I sat there listening to Richie, who obviously was under some kind of influence, drone on and on for nearly an hour. If he sang that night, I don't remember it. I only recall his seemingly endless monologue, which I probably would have considered profound and insightful under other circumstances. But all I could think at the time was: *This is boring, unbelievably boring. Is this what I sound like when I pontificate? Maybe none of us knows what we're talking about, and we're all just blowing smoke, so to speak.*

But the clincher was a Frank Zappa concert that I never attended. I had already started to get really scared over the way I felt when I did certain drugs, and I was still wondering if I might be losing my mind. Not to mention the fact that the speed I did on occasion was wreaking havoc on my already wildly irregular heartbeat. But this one evening, I pulled out all the stops on my physical reaction to drugs. The guy I was seeing at the time, part of this group of friends I'd hooked up with, had apparently moved heaven and earth to get tickets to see Zappa at the Academy of Music in Philly.

We stopped to grab something to eat on the way, but just before we reached the Walt Whitman Bridge, I had a major panic attack. I was dying, and I knew it. My right hand felt like it was frozen solid; my left hand felt like it was on fire. My friend pulled off the highway, and somehow I convinced him I was about to die. He was just as wrecked as I was, so he believed me, turned the car around, and drove back to South Jersey. About halfway home, I came down from whatever I was on, and it hit me: I'd had an ice-cold Stewart's Root Beer mug in my right hand, and my left hand was resting on the car's hot console. The combination, of course, is what accounted for one cold hand and one hot hand. I was not dying after all, just confronted once again with the reality that I should never, ever do drugs.

My friend took me immediately to the house of an older couple that had opened their lives to our ragtag group and any other strays who happened by. We were loved and cared for and always welcome there, and about the only rule they had was an absolute prohibition against drugs of any sort on their property. They were a hip and loving couple, and they were just the people I needed to see that night.

My date explained to Morgan, the male half of the couple, what had happened, at least as well as he could. He wasn't entirely sure what I was going through, but he knew that if I could be helped, Morgan was the one who could do it. He was right.

Morgan took me off to a room away from the others and started talking to me about—of all things—God. Now, I don't think this guy was a Christian, at least not as I understand the term today. Maybe he was, but he seemed more like what we began to call New Age later on. But he apparently did believe in something beyond the here and now, some being that he called God, and that pretty much blew me away. Nobody I knew believed in God anymore. Not only that, he also started talking about Alcoholics Anonymous. Talk about confused—I hadn't touched a drop of alcohol that night, and to me, A.A. was the kind of group that only the broken-down bums on the streets of New York and Philly would join.

It must have taken Morgan an hour to get me to see the connection between God and a higher power and alcohol and drugs and me. Like him, he said, I was one of those people who should never do anything that was even remotely addictive. And in what might seem to be a strange remark to anyone else, he told me there was no shame in that, that I could say no to drugs and alcohol without feeling humiliated. Morgan was the first person to ever give me permission to be straight, without guilt. He was dead-on about my addictive personality.

he punishment that I had secretly hoped would bring me to my senses hit me with full force in the summer of 1970. The semester at the community college had ended, and I was working at a store called Two Guys, a forerunner of the Targets and Kmarts and Wal-Marts that would eventually drive Two Guys out of business. This one Saturday, I was going about my usual routine at work, straightening the shelves and racks in the clothing department and working the cash register when needed. Along about midday, I began to sense that something weird was going on. On a typical Saturday, I'd see lots of people I knew, but on this particular day, more people than usual were looking at me funny. I'd start to get the willies, and I'd look up to find a familiar face staring at me from off in the distance. By the end of my shift, I was feeling decidedly spooked.

ᘒᘒ ᘒᘒ ᘒᘒ

IT WASN'T UNTIL I GOT HOME that I discovered why. My sister called, gauged my ignorance, and then broke the news: Ian, my onetime boyfriend, my forever friend, had been killed in a car crash the night before. Our relationship had been unusual; after dating for a year or so and even talking about marriage, we painlessly segued from a romantic relationship to a brother-sister relationship. I had always felt that whoever I married was simply going to have to accept my friendship with Ian. No wonder so many people were looking at me funny, as I cheerfully went through my day at work, unaware that my soul mate was gone.

By the summer of 1970, kids my age had lost so many of our peers to car crashes that some of us may have mistakenly thought we were immune to any more grief. With so many guys going to Vietnam, we lived with the possibility of death every day. Then there was the occasional freaky death, like the time the lifeless body of one of my sister's friends was found lying in the snow or the too frequent times when couples died of carbon monoxide poisoning as they made out in closed cars in the dead of winter.

But this was Ian, and Ian was not allowed to die before I did. He was always going to be there for me, to protect me. Whenever I thought of him, I thought of the Cat Stevens song "Wild World." I could almost imagine Ian writing that song for me.

I had last seen Ian some seven months earlier. He had dropped out of Monmouth and enlisted in the Coast Guard, where there was less chance of being sent to Vietnam. He was about to be shipped off to Antarctica, and I offered to drive him to New York to see him off at the docks.

But first, we had some serious partying to do, because he wouldn't be home until June at the earliest. It was November, and it was cold in the city, but we walked around Greenwich Village as if it was midsummer, ducking into an occasional bar when the wind got to be too much. Ian couldn't exactly report for duty in a visibly inebriated state, but that didn't stop me from indulging. Ever protective of me, Ian managed to keep me comparatively sober that night. Every now and then, I'd catch him looking at me with that piercing "You don't need to live this way" look that he had. And then an hour or so before he had to report for duty, in a quiet corner of some Village watering hole, he asked me once again to marry him.

We had not dated for more than a year. We were friends, buddies, brother and sister by choice. His proposal seemed to come out of nowhere, and yet it was obvious he had planned it. He was sober, and he was asking me to marry him. I have no idea how I responded, except that my answer was not yes. The circumstances were not conducive to clarity of thought. Here was my good friend, about to leave for the bottom of the world, dropping a bombshell on me that I would have the next seven months to think about.

We dropped the subject almost as quickly as he brought it up. He knew better than to expect an answer, and we agreed to talk about it again when he came home. Over a 3 A.M. breakfast at a coffee shop on the edge of the Village, we also agreed that it would be best if he took the subway to the dock. We were both wrung out emotionally, and a quick good-bye on the street was definitely in order.

We wrote to each other regularly. He'd send me pictures of penguins he befriended; I'd make vague promises about giving serious consideration to his proposal.

Ian was killed on his first night home from Antarctica, when the car he was riding in smacked into a tree at a place on the road from Atlantic City that we called dead man's curve, because so many fatal crashes occurred there.

I hung back in the background at the funeral, in stunned bewilderment. This wasn't supposed to happen; how was I expected to get through life in one piece without Ian? He was the anchor that more than once had kept the boat of my life from drifting out into deeper water than I could handle. I'd even had a few "what the heck" moments during his absence when I thought it might actually make sense for us to marry. He was going to be part of my future anyway, and what were the chances that I'd find someone to marry who would accept Ian as part of the package? Ian loved me, Ian would be faithful to me, and Ian and I had long ago settled the issue of how many children we'd have. While our other friends at the funeral shed their temporary tears, I choked back the sheer terror of facing the future without the one stable person in my life.

Over the next few weeks, friends from Monmouth who couldn't make it to the funeral came to visit, none of them even remotely aware of the depth of my loss. But Ian's parents knew, and I spent many an afternoon with them. And somehow, Herr Muenzer knew;

I saw it in his eyes when we ran into each other in a store. As we reminisced about Ian, the tears that formed in his eyes showed the compassion he had for me.

The combination of Morgan's talking-to and Ian's death forced me to look at what I was doing to myself. Morgan's observations had been accurate, and without Ian around to rein me in, I began to suspect that I was a bona fide goner. Though I didn't recognize it at the time, there was also an unseen hand restraining me.

ᎦᏍᎦᏍᎦ

WHEN I RETURNED TO MONMOUTH for what would have been my junior year, which was actually something like sophomore-plus, I needed that restraining hand like never before. During my missed semester there, some of my friends had introduced a new word to our drug lexicon—*heroin*. The very sound of the word made me tremble. I couldn't believe what I was hearing, that these kids had progressed, or degenerated, to that level. But just as quickly as heroin appeared, it was replaced by what my friends perceived to be a safer drug, cocaine. I never indulged in either, and I was never knowingly in the presence of anyone who was indulging at the time. This one thing I knew: It was time to find a new group of friends.

At first, my new friends were of the literary variety. Though I was hardly what you'd call straight or sober, I was straighter and more sober than I'd been in years. And I began to realize that the field I had chosen—English—was really pretty cool. I found myself reading literature apart from my class assignments—Shakespeare and such for the heck of it.

I fell in love with men by the names of Wordsworth and Whitman, Cowper and Coleridge, Browning and Blake. And even women! Christina Rossetti and the other Browning, but never—never!—Emily Dickinson. I had visibly rattled my English teacher in high school by expressing my opinion that her "poetry"—if you could even call it that—belonged on the pages of *Good Housekeep-ing* magazine. I was not about to recant.

And then there was Dostoevsky and Tolstoy and Kafka and Chekhov, and especially Bertolt Brecht, whose plays I read in German just for fun, even though I was hardly fluent and had to struggle like crazy with it. But this was living! I couldn't believe my good fortune, that I had decided to major in a field that I was suddenly feeling passionate about. Somehow, I had forgotten the passion that had led me to English three years earlier. It was as if I had awakened out of a long and unsatisfying slumber. The circuitry in my brain had reconnected on a higher level.

That meant I was also ready to fall in love with philosophy, with Kant and Kierkegaard and Wittgenstein with his awful blue and brown books, which I never understood but delighted in dissecting all the same. Here were men, mostly, who were trying to sort out the meaning of life, and most of them didn't even go to church. Until I began taking higher-level courses, I never gave much thought to the fact that there were all these philosophers out there who operated outside the confines of the church. There had been Plato and Aristotle and lots of other Greeks, of course, but look what happened to their culture.

☙☙ ☙☙ ☙☙

BY NOW, I WAS LIVING ALONE in a rooming house, having abandoned the cokeheads and finding no one with whom I'd want to share an apartment. The other tenants in the rooming house, less than a block from the beach in Long Branch, were a motley crew: a loquacious guy named Marty, who was either a business or a science major, I never figured out which; a certified pyromaniac who set several fires in the building during his short-lived stay; some long-distance trucker who made spaghetti sauce with tuna instead of meat; and two other students, both women, both relatively normal.

I hit it off with one of those two women right away, even though Gail was a nursing student. Maybe it was because my sister was a nurse, but for whatever reason, I had always placed nurses in a different category. I guess I figured that I could be related to one but not friends with one. Then too, they were into the healing arts, and I was not in any mood to be healed. They were the enemy, in a sense, because they wore white and made you get your drugs legally and thought you had to have a legitimate reason to take them in the first place.

Gail wasn't like that, not like an enemy, that is. She was genuinely friendly and never passed judgment on what the rest of us— meaning me—might be doing. I attributed her cheerful personality to her profession and the fact that she hadn't started working in it yet and therefore hadn't become jaded and grouchy.

One day, I caught her reading her Bible. This was too weird; because she was in nursing school, it wasn't as if she was reading it for World Lit class. Nobody I knew read the Bible. I asked her about it and in doing so stepped right up to the threshold of a dimension I knew I could never enter, given my last encounter with God.

Gail told me she was a Christian, as if that was the most normal thing in the world for a person to say.

"Do you really believe all that?" I asked in astonishment.

She laughed and affirmed that yes, she did indeed believe all that, that Jesus was just as relevant today as He had been two thousand years ago.

She prayed; she had a personal relationship with Jesus; she had to be nuts.

Once I got over the initial shock, I decided not to hold her faith against her, and we continued to hang out together. She didn't do drugs, and I suppose she had an occasional drink, though I don't remember that. Mostly, she just listened and talked and answered my questions and offered advice only when I asked for it.

Meanwhile, I continued to read my favorite poets, apparently unaware on a conscious level that they all wrote blatantly spiritual poetry. Then there was Blaise Pascal's *Pensées*, which I read over and over again. I was well aware of the religious content, but it simply did not occur to me to connect the dots between my attraction to Blake and Donne and Pascal and Dante and Hopkins.

That is, until I met Francis Thompson. I saw myself in his "Hound of Heaven," fleeing God "down the nights and down the days . . . / down the labyrinthine ways / of my own mind: and in the mist of tears / I hid from Him, and under running laughter." Just like that, Thompson—or rather, God—nailed me. But why? This was the same God who had turned His back on me, and here He was, dogging me again. Was this some kind of cruel punishment? Was He feigning an interest in me, working overtime to get my hopes up only to reject me again? I couldn't handle another one of His rejections, that much I knew. But still, the "Hound of Heaven," both the poem and the Person, wouldn't go away.

What I needed was a break from all this heavy philosophical and literary and religious stuff, so when Gail suggested we go skiing, I jumped at the chance. A friend of ours, along with his brother and another guy, invited us to share expenses with them on a three-day trip to Vermont. That sounded good to us, though we soon discovered what the word "share" meant in their little world.

We drove to Manhattan with our friend—I'll call him Ted—and there we picked up big brother "Steve" and his friend "Gary." Without acknowledging our presence in the car, Steve asked Ted if we had paid him and if we had brought along our share of the groceries, which we soon learned meant "more than enough for everybody." So things didn't exactly get off to a great start, but we shrugged it off. We did appreciate the opportunity to go with them.

The weekend, though, went downhill from there. We quickly figured out that we had been invited along to lug stuff into the chalet from the car, make the beds, cook the meals, clean up after the meals, and basically perform all manner of housekeeping functions while the guys skied. Gail and I didn't even bother going to the slopes the last day; we stayed behind just so we could get away from Steve, who warned us not to steal anything while he was gone. We found out later that these guys invited a different group of women to the chalet each time they went, just so they'd have someone along to do their work for them. The whole situation had literally made me sick, and I spent the final day dealing with a stomach virus.

And into the midst of that weekend from hell, God chose to make His most dramatic personal appearance to date.

On our way home—before we had gotten more than a mile or so from the chalet—the guys decided to stop at a country store to buy gifts for their girlfriends, who presumably were smart enough not to go along on these weekend jaunts. Eager for some fresh air, I walked around behind the store, out by the Dumpster and the loading dock. And as I stood there, looking out over the snow-and-evergreen-covered mountains, reality fell away once again, and I found myself in the center of a completely spiritual dimension. The scene before me became misty and blurred, but I was seeing with a greater clarity than ever before. I knew, I *knew* that God was more real than anything I'd ever known or ever would know. I also knew that if He could make Himself so real to me under the circumstances of that weekend, then I could never again doubt His existence or His ability and willingness to reveal Himself to ordinary people like me.

As further proof of God's existence, Gail and I made it home without placing a hex on the guys. The gifts for the girlfriends turned out to be life-sized stuffed animals, which they stuffed into the back seat with us. And after assuring us that we'd be back at Monmouth that same night, they drove instead to somebody's house in North Jersey, where the guys got the bedrooms and the living room. Gail and I were sent down to the cold, unfinished basement to sleep with two enormous, flea-infested, stinky dogs, under thin and musty quilts. We left for Monmouth in the morning, when Ted was good and ready to get up, long after our first classes of the day were over. I wanted to find their car keys and leave in the middle of the night, but Gail talked me out of that temptation. If it hadn't been for her calming influence, we might all have ended up in jail on domestic violence charges.

Ultimately, even the injustice of that last night failed to anger me. Somewhere along the line, it occurred to me that the experience I'd had with God was superior to anything I'd experienced with drugs, and that made the humiliation of that whole weekend worthwhile. I was finished with drugs.

CHAPTER 11

*B*y the spring of 1971, this whole thing with God was starting to heat up. He'd allowed me to have that mystical experience in Vermont, onto which I placed a Cartesian spin: I transcend, therefore I am . . . worthwhile. And there I was, face to face every day with Gail, a walking, talking, believing Christian who still had a brain and a personality. But I couldn't shake the memory of the way God had turned His back on me when I had finally mustered up the courage to seek help two years before.

ᎧᎧ ᎧᎧ ᎧᎧ

MEANWHILE, ONE OF MY CLOSEST FRIENDS—I'll call her Lorraine— discovered she was pregnant. Just about every woman I knew was on the pill at that time, but Lorraine had a serious medical condition that made it impossible for her to take oral contraceptives. It also made it extremely dangerous for her to bear a child.

We hadn't had much contact with each other during the school year—she had left Monmouth a year or so earlier—but our friendship was such that she called to ask me the ultimate favor: to take her to Manhattan to have an abortion. At that time, New York was one of the few states that had legalized the procedure. I considered her request the ultimate favor because it showed she trusted me not to tell anyone; we were all trying to sort out our feelings and opinions on abortion at the time, and she had no way of knowing how I felt about it; and her medical condition made abortion a risky gamble. If anything went wrong, there was a considerable chance that the baby wasn't the only one who would not survive the day. I would be left with the unimaginable responsibility of breaking the news to her parents that their daughter had been pregnant and lost her life trying to reverse that situation. And I didn't even know the father's name or how to reach him; all I knew was that he wanted nothing to do with this child.

Lorraine's tenuous condition meant that she would need special monitoring and more recovery time than the typical abortion patient, so the staff advised me to wait several hours before returning. Once I left the hospital, I was at a loss. Even for me, 10 A.M. was a bit early to be hanging out in a bar, but these were unusual circumstances. I headed for one of the many Irish taverns—dives, to be precise—that surrounded the hospital on the Upper West Side.

I went inside, and once my eyes adjusted to the dim light and my nose adjusted to air that was heavy with the sickly smell of hard liquor, I realized I was the only woman in the place, and almost the only customer. I must have looked particularly hippie-ish, because Mr. O'Malley or Mr. O'Brien or Mr. O'Shaughnessy, whoever the proprietor was, took an immediate dislike to me, snarling at me in the way the Establishment snarled at all of us at that time. I wondered if the only other customer, a man, was waiting out his wife's labor. The place almost certainly would have drawn its clientele from those who had business at the hospital. Maybe this customer was waiting for someone to be released or for visiting hours to start or for an unborn baby to die.

I nursed my beer, or rather, my beers, and wondered if the demons would turn up the flames in hell on me because of this. I shouldn't have been waiting for an abortion patient, shouldn't have been asked to get involved in this mess. The father of the child that had been sentenced to death should have been there to help Lorraine. But what can you expect from a guy who never even called to find out the results of the pregnancy test? I was sick, sick at the thought of what Lorraine was going through, but also sick that I had been drawn into this and that I had to confront this whole abortion thing head-on.

I hadn't thought much about the abortion issue before, but I spent that morning in as serious a time of reflection as I'd ever had. My head argued, *She couldn't have carried the baby to term—she almost certainly would have died.* My heart responded, *I feel ill.* Head: *Besides, the father abandoned her, and she couldn't raise the baby by herself.* Heart: *She could have put the baby up for adoption.* Head: *But what about her parents?* Heart: *But what about forgiveness?*

Once my internal bickering ended, I was left with one feeling in my gut, and only one: This was wrong, really and truly wrong, though I couldn't articulate why. And it stopped mattering that I couldn't.

At a Schrafft's restaurant, buoyed no doubt by its classiness compared to O'Malley's or O'Brien's or O'Shaughnessy's or whatever, I switched to wine and some kind of after-dinner drink, only it was lunchtime and just barely at that. And I was the one driving. Maybe I was asking for trouble, but I couldn't face a post-op Lorraine without a few more drinks under my belt. The waitress at Schrafft's took me under her waitstaff wings and tried to comfort me, undoubtedly a skill required of the crew at this particular site. Yes, I told her, I was visiting someone at the hospital, someone who was dying. That was the only way I could explain the tears I kept trying to hold back.

Lorraine came through fine, if you can apply the word *fine* to an exceedingly complex situation that involves deceiving your family, obliterating a life, and wrestling with demons and angels. We were both fine, just fine, thank you.

෬ ෬ ෬

As was my habit when things got too intense, I moved once again. My job cleaning tables in the college cafeteria would be over at the end of the school year, so it was time to head for Asbury Park, six miles south and loaded with summer job opportunities. I tried to get a job as a waitress—honest, I really did—but ended up as a barmaid. It didn't matter that I was slightly underage; I was willing to wear hot pants, those ultrashort shorts that we wore with knee-high suede boots back then, and I'd be turning twenty-one soon enough. I was hired.

The money was good, even in the seedy places where I worked. The biggest tip I ever got, or could have had, was a trip to Copenhagen, except I would have had to go with the customer who offered the tip. I declined that one.

In one place where I worked, the mob was quietly evident. It took a while, but I finally figured out what was going on. A few of my customers would pull up in the parking lot in beat-up old cars—never together, by the way—come in, spend money like crazy, and leave a huge tip. I'd look at them, look at their wads of cash, look at their crummy cars, and try to make sense of it all. Then someone tipped me off, someone who worked nearby and was known to be connected to the mob. "Shut up!" he whispered to me when I asked why these rich guys drove such lousy cars. "They want to keep a low profile when they come in here. Do you want to get us all killed?" Good grief, one of those guys had taken me out for expensive dinners several times after my shift behind the bar ended. He'd been polite and respectful and never made a move toward me. He figured I was a struggling college kid—he was right about that—and he wanted to make sure I had a good meal now and then. And here he was a hit man, with eighteen kills to his name, at last count. I wasn't what you'd call a good judge of character in those days.

And I still wasn't a good judge of my limitations where alcohol was concerned. In reality, I had zero tolerance for alcohol, but I wouldn't admit it. All it took was one drink to set me off on an all-night or all-weekend drinking binge. I never drank while I was working, but I more than made up for those few hours of sobriety. I became something of an authority on the fastest-acting hangover cures and the best foods to eat while you were drinking.

Not surprisingly, I found myself drawn to the works of authors like Camus and Sartre. The bleaker the outlook on life, the more I could relate to it. Sartre's anguished view of reality was right up my alley.

From existentialist France, it was a very short walk to Marxist Russia.

One of my drinking buddies, a history professor, was an outspoken Marxist, and toward the end of the school year, he'd amassed quite a following among the student body. We would get together at his apartment or a local bar and listen to him regale us with delightful readings from the works of the ever-chipper Karl Marx. Good heavens, I don't know what we were thinking. If you weren't suffering from existential angst or chronic depression at the start of the evening, you would be by midnight. Those should have been sobering experiences, but they just drove me to drink all the more, before, during, and after the readings.

This was all the perfect setup for what I suspected were the final days of my short life.

CHAPTER 12

The day I decided to kill myself was a Thursday. That wasn't the day I was going to do it; that was just the day I made the decision. The actual date of my planned demise was sometime in the future, a date entirely dependent on my parents and their respective deaths. That made perfect sense to me at the time.

☙☙ ☙☙ ☙☙

THE TIME, OTHER THAN THURSDAY, was late that summer, the summer of 1971. Now that I had turned twenty-one, I was in all ways and in all states a legal adult. I could do as I pleased, and I pleased to end my life. Was I suicidal? Well, yes, except for the fact that I hated that word. It was so fraught with high-strung emotion; it positively reeked of hysteria, and that wasn't at all what I felt. Life wasn't working, and I was banking on the afterlife to be a major improvement. It was that simple.

Where I got my sophisticated view of the afterlife at that time I don't know. All I know is that somewhere along the line I had picked up this notion that when I died I'd be transformed into a spirit floating above the earth. I'd be able to recognize the spirits of my dearly departed friends, if and when we happened to bump into each other. It all sounded so peaceful and ethereal, and I took it as gospel.

I don't know who I thought these "dearly departed friends" would be; I had never been so bereft of friends as I was that summer, with all my college friends gone until the fall. Unless, of course, you counted Mrs. Schultz, the resident senior citizen at the rundown hotel where I worked as a barmaid, or Linda, the official hotel prostitute who met her clients in the bar, with its swashbuckling name, the Buccaneer Room. You certainly couldn't count the guy I was seeing at the time, a self-described free spirit, or the nice hit man, the one I went out to dinner with on several occasions before discovering his career choice. Or the old Romanian palm reader who cooked cabbage in her room down the hall from mine, on the third floor of a dilapidated rooming house in Asbury Park. On the bright side, I could sit on my bed, look out the window at her fortune-telling booth on the boardwalk, and predict when she'd come home and start cooking again.

So I had no real friends, but as usual, I found myself in the company of misfits.

On that Thursday night in 1971, my boyfriend was off being a free spirit, and I didn't feel like hitting the bars by myself. As I stared out at the honky-tonk activity on the boardwalk, the meaning of my life suddenly hit me: *You were destined to live a squalid existence. It's never going to get any better than this. Either get used to it or get out.*

I was already so used to it that it made me sick, so I decided to get out. I sat there on the bed, listening to the Moody Blues and the organ-grinding din of the Jersey Shore, and convinced myself that even after I graduated from college, even after I became a teacher and started getting a real paycheck, things would not be any better. My life stretched out before me like a big, gaping, everlasting yawn. I wanted out.

I had two problems, though, namely, my mother and father. If I killed myself, I'd end up killing them; I assumed they'd immediately drop dead of grief. At first, I reasoned that that wouldn't really matter to me, of course, because I would be dead and gone and wouldn't know anything about it. And it hadn't occurred to me yet that I'd have a tough time looking their spirits in the eye if we happened to bump into each other as we floated above the earth.

In the end, it was my heightened view of justice and personal rights that won out; I had every right to take my own life, but I had no right to cause their deaths in the process. So I postponed my suicide and waited for other people to die.

In the meantime, I knew that I needed to refine my understanding of life after death. This floating-spirit idea was starting to bother me, though I wasn't sure why. Once classes resumed in the fall, I spent my spare time in the college library reading up on other religions—anything other than Christianity.

I was still convinced that God was real, but I could not shake the memory of His outright rejection of me. The real God didn't want me, but I figured there were all these lesser gods who would recruit me in a heartbeat. Before I signed up, though, I wanted to know what I was getting into, so I took up residence at the extreme ends of Dewey's 200 aisle at the Guggenheim Library. Hinduism was a front-runner for a while, but I knew I could never keep all their gods straight; I mean, there were thousands of them, and I didn't have that much time left to sort them all out. I finally settled on Baha'i, but halfheartedly. Baha'i didn't make much more sense than any other religion did, but Seals & Crofts were Baha'i, and maybe they'd explain it all to me through their music. It was a theory that sounded all right at the time.

That is, until Christmas break. For some reason, that year— maybe it was to check on the health of my parents, I don't know—I decided to go home a few days earlier than usual. There I hooked up with a couple of old friends, particularly one who had always reminded me of Bob Dylan. He was sort of quiet and reclusive, and he kept the town well stocked with an assortment of controlled dangerous substances.

It was in his house that I was introduced to out-and-out Satanic rock music. I knew there were those who thought that all rock music was of the devil, and there was lots of music that spoke of the devil in overt ways. But this was the real thing—an entire album titled *Witchcraft*, recorded, as I recall, by an actual coven. Rock songs praising Satan filled one side; a complete black mass filled the other.

At first, I was mildly frightened by what I was hearing—not just on the album but also in what "Dylan" and another friend were saying. They both believed all this, that it was all right to embrace evil and give yourself over to Satan. We argued—intellectually and philosophically, of course—about it for hours. When I left his house that night, I was unconvinced but definitely intrigued.

The following night, it was as if a light went on in my brain—a cliché, for sure, but one that perfectly describes what happened. Except, of course, that it was darkness that crept in, merely disguised as light. Anyway, the darkness disguised as light came in the form of a question: *Why am I messing with these lesser gods and prophets, namely Baha'u'llah at the moment, when I can go straight to the number two power in the universe—Satan himself?*

I went right out and bought the *Witchcraft* album, a bizarre Christmas gift if there ever was one. When I returned to college after the holidays, my parents were still breathing, and I had worn a permanent groove in my new favorite album.

☙☙ ☙☙ ☙☙

I HADN'T COUNTED ON GETTING blindsided by God first thing in the new year. He came looking a whole lot like the Monmouth College track team, and He—or they—ran right over me as I inched my way ever closer to a complete surrender to Satan. It all started in January, when one of the guys found Jesus.

Talk about betrayal. Some of the team members lived in the same rooming house where the palm reader and I lived, and we all paid our rent to the track coach, who owned the building. We had worked out a reasonable arrangement, one based on the same idea behind the "Don't ask, don't tell" policy that the government finally caught on to several decades later. We were all engaged in various questionable activities, some illegal, some just immoral. But we kept our mouths shut. The last thing we needed was a Jesus freak, a potential whistleblower to be sure. We couldn't trust him anymore.

Then, a month later, the unthinkable happened: A second guy became a religious fanatic. He was even worse than the first; he came right out and told me he was praying for my salvation. I was all for personal freedom, and he could do whatever he liked, but I was hopping mad that he was trying to get me involved. What did he know? He had no idea that God and I had already parted ways for good; all he knew was that I had this Satanic album, and for some reason, he thought that explained everything. Well, he could pray for me if he wanted to, but it wasn't going to change a thing. And I told him as much. He just smiled and walked away, and I wanted to break his running legs.

By March, the two evangelists had gotten to a third guy on the team.

I did the only logical thing I could think to do: I left the country. So that was a bit drastic, I admit, and I came back from my Canadian vacation soon enough, but I couldn't stand the rooming house any longer. One by one, the tenants were becoming Christians. I didn't like the way this whole thing was racing through the building.

So I moved out, leaving the palm reader to fend for herself. The Jesus freaks had borrowed my *Witchcraft* album and then burned it; for a while, I amused myself imagining how they were going to hoodwink a fortune-teller into handing over the tools of her trade.

Maybe they had acquired a few new skills as they tried to convert her, because somehow they tracked me down in my new place, a room I was renting from the mother of a bellhop I knew from the hotel. Like clockwork, every Friday afternoon in April, one of the three runners—Glen, Chris, or Steve—would call and invite me to attend a Christian meeting that night.

And like clockwork, I would say no, but not because I had anything better to do. My '61 Renault had bit the dust; I had ditched the free spirit; and while I was out of the country, a former friend had taken my bartending job. I had nothing, absolutely nothing, not even a way to get to class during the week. But I did not want anything the Jesus freaks were offering, because I knew what they didn't: No matter what they believed, salvation was not available to everyone.

CHAPTER 13

W hat happened next I can only attribute to ennui and spring fever. I was going stir-crazy in my little room, miles from the boardwalk and far too many blocks from the kind of bar I'd normally frequent. There were no parties going on, nothing to do that first weekend in May 1972. I had stayed home all day and all night on Thursday, giving anybody who desired the pleasure of my company ample opportunity to call and invite me out somewhere. Here it was Friday afternoon, and no one had phoned—not even Glen, or Chris, or Steve. In my desperation, I called Glen. If he thought he was going to get by without inviting me to go to his Friday night Christian meeting, he had another think coming.

◉◉ ◉◉ ◉◉

HE TOLD ME WHAT TIME HE'D COME by to pick me up. Great. Now I was in trouble, big trouble. Why couldn't I have kept my mouth shut? Would it really have been all that hard to stay home on a Friday night for once in my life? What was I thinking?

I worked up a nasty attitude just in time for Glen's arrival. I got in the car, slunk down in the seat, and basically sulked all the way to the Ocean Front House, a onetime rooming house on the Ocean Grove beach that was now home to a communal group of Christian guys. As he parked the car, Glen looked at me funny and asked, "So are you going to get saved tonight?"

Saved? Me? No way! I was only there under the duress of boredom. But I muttered, "I don't know" and hoped Glen couldn't see how nervous I had suddenly become. The evening hadn't even officially started, and already I was a wreck.

I'm sure I was glowering as we walked in, and naturally, everybody in the room looked at me funny, just the way Glen had. Someone offered me a chair, but I shook my head and sat on the floor. Everyone around me was laughing and talking and having a great time, but I just sat there checking out the intricate weave of the fibers in the carpet. The others left me alone, no doubt aware that I would have barked had anyone spoken to me. I was acting like the quintessential female dog.

Someone—the leader, I guess—started to speak, and the room got very quiet. I managed to look up and started checking out this well-scrubbed pack of college kids. I decided I hated every last one of them, especially the Barbie-and-Ken duo sitting on the sofa across from me. Barbie was oh-so-perfect, with her flawless complexion and surfer-blonde hair and bright blue eyes and straight white teeth. And Ken, her adoring companion, was just as pretty. My, my, didn't those two look like they'd just stepped out of a Mattel toy box? *Gee, I wonder what they'll wear to the prom.*

For the next hour, I analyzed and passed judgment on every person in the room except my three friends, because I'd analyzed and judged them months earlier. These Christians, I decided, were pure plastic, artificial replicas of real people. What did they know about life? The only reason they could sit there and smile their sickening Christian smiles was because they'd never been where I'd been or done what I'd done. And what could they possibly know about God? They had probably been good little children all their lives, so they couldn't know what it felt like to have God turn His back on them.

And the speaker: Where did they get this guy from? He rides up on a motorcycle and claims to be a professor at some Christian college in North Jersey. The group was utterly delighted to have him there that night, and they all sat listening attentively as he droned on and on about God and Jesus and the Bible. I scowled at every available opportunity.

The only sentence I recall him saying that night was this: "God not only forgave your sins, He forgot them." It was a simple nine-word sentence that changed my life.

Who can possibly predict what precise combination of words will strike at the heart of a person's inmost being? Why did I believe that those particular words were true, when for years I had labored under the belief that I was beyond hope of salvation? To this day, I cannot explain what made me think the professor's words applied to me, on that night, in that place. What I do know is that his words struck me like a hammer blow, shattering the hardened shell that I had formed around myself as I sat on the floor that night. And that's not an image I'm superimposing today on an event that happened decades ago; that's how I felt that night.

Chris was sitting on the floor next to me, and as soon as the biker prof stopped speaking, I asked him if we could go out on the porch and talk. As we sat down on the rocking chairs outside, Chris made some offhand comment about how beautiful the night was—and it was beautiful, with the reflected light of a full moon in turn reflected on the unusually calm ocean. But there would be no conversation that night. The last word I spoke as an unredeemed, lost soul was Chris's name. Collapsing in his arms, I sobbed up every last defense, every last excuse, every last grievance against God, without uttering a single word. As Chris prayed, I entered familiar territory, the same spiritual dimension I had experienced in Vermont. The moment was much too fleeting, but this time it came with an unmistakable identifying mark: love. For an all-too-brief space of time, I sensed that I was in the presence of pure love.

Later, of course, I said the obligatory sinner's prayer; there was no way that crew would let me out the door that night without hearing me utter the Christian mantra. But everything God needed to accomplish in my life He accomplished as I sat on the porch, wordlessly embracing all that He had to offer. Forgiveness topped the list.

I knew, without a doubt, that He had forgiven me for everything, for walking away from Him and making a shambles of my life, for hurting and endangering others with my reckless behavior, for squandering the love He had lavished on me.

Someone wisely made note of the time and suggested I write the hour and the date in my Bible. I was too overcome by the newness of my reconciliation with God to appreciate the wisdom of this, but I later did as he suggested. For years to come, I was grateful for that one bit of advice, because the doubt that I could not even imagine at that moment would plague me countless times.

In fact, my first moment of serious doubt was only hours away, before I even had a chance to buy a Bible in which to document the time and date. Back in my room that same night, I faced the terrorizing thought that maybe I hadn't done this whole thing just right, that now I had to "ask Jesus to come into my heart," using those very words, or else I would be doomed all over again. So I said those words repeatedly, hoping that my repeated requests would finally make some kind of impression on God, I suppose. In the middle of all this vain repetition, the doorbell rang, which did nothing to endear me to my landlady, because it was 1 A.M. It was my three friends, God bless their discerning spirits, come to assure me that what had happened to me on the porch earlier that night was real and valid and pleasing to God. They had stopped by because they knew how suddenly the doubts could come and take root. In the future, whenever I led someone into the presence of God for the first time, I followed my friends' example. In every case, I found that those new believers had also faced immediate doubts.

The timing of my entrance into the kingdom of God could not have been better, in one way at least. I thought it would have been a whole lot better if all this had happened a year or ten earlier, naturally, but the time of year was perfect. The school year was coming to a close, and I had no opportunity to become annoyingly and cluelessly evangelistic with my friends at Monmouth. God made sure they were safely gone for summer vacation before I could unleash my ignorant zeal on them.

And zealous I was, to be sure. In all fairness, I recognize that the initial zeal of a new believer is to be expected, as painful as it can be to its victims. Here I was, a walking, talking paradox, washed in the blood and clean as a whistle, all the sins I'd chalked up completely erased from God's memory. Who wouldn't want to shout this brand of Good News from the housetops of Asbury Park?

I shouted the news first of all to Gail, with whom I had kept in touch throughout her many interstate moves. She was back at home in Ohio for a few weeks but told me she would be returning to New Jersey in time for the big Explo Christian rally, which was going to be held in Texas.

"Uh, OK, but what does an event in Texas have to do with us?" I asked.

"Well, we can go together," she suggested. Never mind that neither of us had a car or a job or any other Christian friends that we could hitch a ride with. If God wants us there, we'll get there, she assured me.

Well, now, this was a whole new function of faith that I'd never heard of before. All we had to do was place our trust in Jesus, and He'd get us wherever we wanted to go, though secretly I knew I was placing my trust not in Jesus but in Gail's trust in Jesus. She knew the ropes and spoke so confidently that I let her orchestrate the whole thing.

Which is how we came to cause a minor accident between two semis less than an hour after our excellent adventure got under way. That's because all of Gail's efforts to find a ride to Dallas had failed, and she decided we would hitchhike. Two young women. From North Jersey to Texas. Without one complete weapon between us. Hey, it was 1972, and everyone was hitchhiking. Not everyone was reaching their destination alive or intact, but Gail was convinced God would protect us.

It was chilly the morning we left, so we were pretty well covered up, with hooded sweatshirts and all. As we stood on the side of some highway in New Jersey, our thumbs out in typical hitchhiker fashion, several semis pulled up to the red light at the intersection where we stood. The driver of one truck apparently noticed that we weren't exactly guys, did a double take, and forgot to hit the brake. It was a minor accident, and we tried really hard not to laugh, but I wondered if this was some kind of omen of things to come on this trip.

As it turned out, most of the people who picked us up were exceedingly kind to us, offering a few dollars or buying us a meal. More than one was a parent whose own offspring was out on the road somewhere, relying on the kindness of strangers to get them where they wanted to go. We thought we were in big trouble when an off-duty Ohio state trooper picked us up, but it turned out he just wanted to see us safely to our destination. When he found out our destination was Dallas, though, he had second thoughts and dropped us off in Terre Haute, Indiana.

Had he known how our next ride would go, he might have driven us all the way to Dallas after all. Because two guys picked us up, and by all appearances they were not the kind you'd want your daughter to live in the same state with, let alone get in a car with. But we did get in the car, and only when it was too late did we realize the implications of riding in a two-door: We were trapped in the back seat. That would even have been all right if we hadn't noticed the gun in the front seat. And when they started heading east toward who-knows-where instead of west toward Dallas, we were scared out of our wits.

Gail found her voice before I did and pointed out that we should be heading toward the setting sun, not away from it. Without a word, the driver turned the car around. Now I knew we were dead meat, because we had clearly made him mad.

By then, the day had heated up and so had the guys, who decided what we all needed was to go skinny-dipping. We left the interstate and drove through a desolate area to a gas station, which—surprise, surprise!—happened to be abandoned. While the guys went to get a soda from a nearby vending machine, Gail got out to call the police. The phone in the phone booth was dead, just like we were about to be. Gail climbed back in the car, and as we plotted our next move, the guys returned with one opened bottle of Coke for Gail and me. Thus began my short-lived stint as designated drug tester. We agreed that because I was familiar with the effects of drugs and Gail was not, I would take the first few sips just in case the guys had slipped something into the bottle. We were both hot and thirsty, and sipping that soda took unbearable restraint. I was so miserable that I really didn't care if they had laced it with LSD, but there was Gail to consider.

As I nursed the Coke, the guys drove around trying to find the lake into which we were supposed to dip our skinnies. They never found it. Instead, they drove us to St. Louis, dropped us off, and did not shoot us. They turned around and headed back to Indiana, as if our encounter had been the most normal thing in the world.

The Coke was clean. Gail drank the rest of the bottle. It had been an unusually weird day. To top it off, we slept in sleeping bags on top of picnic tables at a rest stop in Missouri. When we woke up unmolested the following morning, I was finally convinced that God does indeed protect fools.

We made it to Dallas, where the Christians in the city and sub-urbs had opened their homes to the eighty thousand kids who had come to attend Explo, and we found a place to stay in a really nice house in Fort Worth, owned by an equally nice woman. We attended workshops and seminars in various churches during the day and rallies at the Cotton Bowl at night. It was at that stadium, on the final night of Explo '72, that I was numbered among those who could not stand when the speaker asked us to make a no-turning-back commitment to Jesus. I wanted to stand, I really did, but I knew how weak I was, and even after a week of intensive Bible instruction, I was not ready to make a vow to God that I was not sure I could keep.

I wasn't about to let my last-night failure overshadow all the good things I did that week, like memorizing 1 John 1:9 and never forgetting it, and finding a ride all the way to Akron, Ohio. Our ride was in an overcrowded and overheated compact car, and at least one person in the car resented our presence, but because we'd all just come from Explo and we were all supposed to be good Christians, she couldn't make too much of a stink about it.

Safely back in New Jersey—if one can ever be both—I was still in that wonderful honeymoon phase with Jesus, so my bliss-covered eyes hadn't yet focused on all those people who were now looking at me funnier than ever, especially when I tried to entertain them with readings from my newly discovered literary genre, the gospel tract.

Tracts provided a great way for people like me to spread the Good News. I could hand them out and walk away before anyone had a chance to ask me a question or engage me in conversation or challenge my beliefs. Even better, I could surreptitiously place them in rest rooms or other public places, and no one would have to know who placed them there. Stealth evangelism was better than nothing, I figured.

But God help the person who blundered into a discussion with me about my newfound faith. For one thing, they were in for an earful. Even worse, they were in for an earful of questionable doctrine. Because I had spent so much of my early childhood in church, I felt I should be able to answer any challenge and defend any attack. But I was on very shaky ground, relying on my memory of Sunday school and church and vacation Bible school. Even when I started to give an answer that I knew was indefensible—or one that I myself secretly doubted—I rambled on, offering vague explanations and dreading the moment when I'd be back in my seventh-grade classroom, caught giving a clearly wrong answer. All I can say now is that I'm glad God is able to correct the unbelievably foolish things that new believers often say.

I continued attending meetings at the Ocean Front House, where we newcomers were encouraged to find a church. Well, I thought, how hard can that be?

CHAPTER 14

S o there I was, ready to be trained to take on Satan and his demons so we could usher in the kingdom of God. I looked around and discovered a church nearby that sported a familiar word on its outdoor bulletin board—*Baptist*. And my favorite church word—*First*. Some of the kids from the Ocean Front House attended this church, and I knew the Baptist routine even if I was a little bit rusty. From what I had experienced in my childhood, I believed I could count on the Baptists to stick to the Bible and not lead me astray. I was not disappointed; they even baptized me, fully immersing me in a tank full of water as part of a ritual that meant more to me than they could ever know.

౷౷ ౷౷ ౷౷

I REPORTED FOR DUTY AT every Sunday service and every Wednesday night prayer meeting. I attended the college and career Sunday school class and enrolled in the church's Bible institute, through which I took courses in doctrine and Greek and whatever else was offered. But this didn't feel like God's army, at least not the way I expected it to feel. Maybe we didn't exactly take on the kingdom of darkness through heroic exploits, but we did pray and we did believe and we did memorize the Word as a buttress against the time we were certain was coming, the day when it would be against the law for us to own a Bible.

Maybe that sounds like paranoia, and perhaps a bit of that did creep in, but we were preparing, not panicking, and the sense of urgency we carried with us had a beneficial effect: We got to know the Bible inside out, memorizing entire chapters, entire books. We had a solid grounding in the historical pattern of God's plan of redemption. We knew how to find what we needed in the Scriptures, because we had been given a thorough overview of the general themes of each book. If we needed comfort, we'd go to the Psalms; wisdom, to Proverbs; a reason to argue with each other, anything Paul wrote about women.

We were trained in a variety of evangelism techniques, including how to talk to people while we were handing out those delightful little tracts and how to go door-to-door with the gospel without making complete fools of ourselves, a lesson I never mastered. I hated neighborhood evangelism and cringed every time I rang a doorbell. More than one person sat and smirked as I dug a theological hole for myself out of the lethal combination of zeal and ignorance.

Worst of all, in terms of making a fool of myself, was the jail ministry I became involved with. We would go to the county jail every couple of weeks and talk about Jesus to girls who were awaiting trial for offenses like robbery and prostitution. They tolerated us, and one or two seemed to look forward to our visits, probably because we were the only people who came to see them. But even with my dubious past, I was way out of my league. These girls were tougher than I'd ever been, and they had done things I never considered doing. Sure, I could still talk to them about God and tell them about my changed life, but when they turned hostile and started challenging me, I would bluff my way out of the situation with some abstract comment that even I didn't understand, and I would pray for the guard to come and tell us our time was up.

The Baptist services were church as usual, and even though I accepted that, it still bothered me to no end. Having come into the family of God through the Jesus People movement, I knew there were people out there fighting from the trenches, frontline warriors who were taking on giants such as drug addiction and physical abuse and promiscuity and prostitution, and I was sitting in a pew singing nineteenth-century hymns—which, by the way, I love, but which weren't doing a whole lot for the people outside the church, unless of course they happened to walk by and catch the Spirit as we were singing a particularly fetching tune. And that wasn't often.

It was in the midst of this traditional church environment that my vision finally cleared. And that's when I realized that even these kindred spirits, my new brothers and sisters in Christ, were looking at me funny. I didn't dress right; I didn't look right; I didn't talk right. I still had this countercultural aura about me, even though I had cleaned up my act and had tried my very best to look like Barbie, who, by the way, I discovered had once been a street prostitute, so there went the judgment I leveled against everyone at the Ocean Front House the night I was saved.

Some of my most deeply held convictions were about to be compromised, all for the sake of conformity.

෴ ෴ ෴

I DON'T BLAME THE CHURCH—the cultural church as well as individual congregations—for wanting us to conform. It's not easy to keep a motley crew in line; Jesus Himself faced that predicament. I do blame myself and others like me for trying to change our God-given natures to fit in with a human idea of what a Christian should be like. Being a language-oriented person, I learned Christian jargon as a second language in no time at all, and soon I had lost the ability to talk about my faith in actual English. This was conducive neither to spreading the gospel among the English-speaking populace nor to maintaining friendships with normal Americans.

My clothes were the next item on my makeover agenda. I hardly had the means to go out and buy a whole new church-approved wardrobe, and really, my current wardrobe was not at all what you'd call provocative. But I didn't fit in, and God knows I wanted to. So I managed to assemble an appropriate outfit that I wore on every church occasion, until I figured out that wearing the same outfit over and over again branded me as an even more obvious misfit.

This was getting annoying. I'd been living a purposely simplified life—why would anyone need more than two pairs of bell-bottoms and five shirts in their closet?—and I was feeling this pressure to complicate it. After years of being unafraid to express my individuality, I was in danger of becoming a Baptist clone. My sister, in fact, criticized me for becoming a blue-haired old church lady. This was decades before blue hair became trendy and thus was not a compliment. Furthermore, it was well deserved. She was right.

Finally, now that I had changed my vocabulary and was at least working on my appearance, it was time to deal with my behavior. I had given up the overt sins, things like drinking and smoking and partying, but I still didn't act like a Baptist. I was on my final approach to the ecclesiastical twilight zone, that eerie and disorienting realm where man-made rules take on the authority of gospel, where the unspoken pressure to conform threatens to lobotomize you and remove every last vestige of the uniqueness that is you.

I could tell right away that I wouldn't be reading much philosophy anymore, or at least I wouldn't admit it. After all, I had found the truth, and I shouldn't clutter my mind with diverse viewpoints. My life would be orchestrated to revolve around one central theme, the church, and anything that didn't relate to God or the Bible or the church would simply not do.

Deep down, I knew that everything related to God in some way. But I had been indoctrinated into this new and narrow way of believing, and expressing what was deep down inside of me was not going to endear me to my adopted spiritual family. I wanted so much to fit in that I kept my mouth shut, suppressed my natural instincts, and little by little sacrificed pieces of myself to the larger goal of finding acceptance in the church.

Being accepted also meant that it was time to switch the dial on my radio. However, this was one change I made willingly, without argument. I still loved rock and folk and jazz and blues and even a smattering of classical, the one category that was still acceptable. But the familiar songs brought back memories of depravity, and I was more than happy to find an excuse to stop listening to them. The Jesus People had ushered in a whole new music genre, Christian rock, and late at night, I was able to draw in signals from stations on Long Island and in upstate New York that played hip Christian music. During the day, I was stuck with a station that played hymns and Southern gospel and the kind of songs male quartets were required by law to sing. But the station also aired some programs that featured solid biblical teaching, so I persevered.

I may have been willing to switch to Christian music, but I drew the line at getting rid of my old albums. Some kids burned their albums, and if that's what God told them to do, then they had to do it. But He didn't tell me the same thing, although several people did, emphasizing that it would prove my commitment to Jesus, and it would rid my room of anything that I would be ashamed to have Jesus see if He were to visit me. This was a huge concept at the time, that our homes should not contain anything that we would not want the Lord to see if He should drop by for tea or something. At the same time, we were taught that He was omnipresent and omniscient, so He was already in my room and knew what was there, right down to the germs and dust mites that I couldn't even see. Surely He hadn't overlooked my complete Beatles collection. So what was the point in getting rid of it?

No, I would not burn the Moody Blues or Creedence Clearwater Revival or even the Doors, who flat-out begged me to light their fire. This was history, mine and my generation's, and I wasn't going to watch it go up in flames. Or more accurately, melt into a solid vinyl mass.

Neither would I burn my books, as others suggested. The thought of defacing a book in any way, other than the underlining that I had to do to keep my thoughts straight for school, was anathema to me. To this day, I visibly shudder when I see someone dog-ear the page of a book, and I've taken several friends to task for the habit. It's just not in me to burn a book.

I began spending a lot of time at the local Christian bookstore, and being unemployed, I naively wrote down the titles of the books I wanted to read, figuring I could borrow them from the library. Not one title was available at the library, and I gradually caught on to the fact that if the librarians had anything to do with it, none of my selected titles would ever be made available. The best I could do was to find an occasional book by Billy Graham, but that wasn't what I was looking for at the time.

To feed my addiction to books, I set off in hot pursuit of a job and ended up in the most un-Baptist place of all, another bar.

hadn't set out to get a job in a bar. One of my former customers, the kind who drove his old, beat-up car to the bar where I used to work, graciously gave me one of his old, beat-up cars. That '52 Buick drove like a tank, but it got me where I wanted and needed to go. In the fall of 1972, that meant school and work. I had heard that the restaurant at a nearby country club needed waitresses. It was close to where I lived, meaning less wear and tear on the bomb I was driving, so that was a plus.

ᏋᎶ ᏋᎶ ᏋᎶ

THE MANAGER WASN'T TOO THRILLED to find out how limited my serving experience was. This place was mainly a banquet facility that catered to weddings and other special functions; unlike a typical restaurant, there was no slow time when a new waitress could be trained. All the work hours were busy hours.

When he asked about my last job—which I had listed only by the name of the hotel where the bar was located—my heart sank. I reluctantly admitted I'd been a barmaid, and he hired me on the spot. It turned out that they were even more shorthanded behind the bar than they were in the banquet hall. Because I hadn't worked in several months, I felt I couldn't turn down an offer of immediate employment.

I didn't know what to make of this. Remembering how Gail had trusted God with every little detail of her life, I wondered if this was some kind of test, and if so, what kind. Was God seeing if I would trust Him to provide another job, or was He seeing if I would trust Him to keep me sober? I'd like to believe that I was young and innocent and naive, but I'm pretty sure my gut feeling was that I should run in the opposite direction, live in a tent, and eat dirt rather than go back to work in a bar. I took the job anyway, and that decision set in motion a string of events that led to one of the biggest mistakes of my life.

But before I committed this huge mistake, which involved a guy with a sports car and a British accent, I had to put in a lot of hours behind a bar again. I tried my hand at evangelistic bartending, which went over about as well as you'd expect it to. I became increasingly uncomfortable serving drinks to the already drunk, and one night I committed the unpardonable sin: I flagged a regular customer. Not only was he way too drunk to drive, he also was giving me the creeps. So I cut him off—no more beer, no more shots. My days, or nights, as a barmaid were numbered.

Sensing unemployment in my near future, and with only one semester of school left, I started to give some serious thought to getting a real job after graduation. All along, I'd planned on becoming an English teacher, and this final semester, during which I'd do my student teaching practicum, would be instrumental in helping me decide which school system would be the best place to teach. Or so I thought.

I was assigned to teach seventh grade in a school at the Jersey Shore that had a so-so reputation—not bad, but nothing to write home about. The kids did their best to take advantage of me, but I finagled a way to get their ringleader on my side, so I pretty much won out in the end. I discovered, however, that I dreaded the thought of becoming a teacher. I loved teaching, and I loved the kids, but I hated the politics. The other teachers just about drove me nuts, whining and complaining and backbiting and undermining each other. The kids started to look more mature to me than the teachers did. It didn't take a genius to figure out that you couldn't be a teacher without becoming embroiled in petty bickering. I knew I would never fit in; *nonpolitical teacher* was an oxymoron. I finished the semester and my time as a college student more disillusioned than I'd ever been before. I did not have my picture taken for the yearbook. I didn't even attend my own graduation ceremony. My mother earned her G.E.D. that same year, and that seemed a greater cause for celebration.

What now? Two memories converged and prompted me to answer an ad I'd seen in the local paper. The first was the memory of the encounter I'd had with the budding journalist several years earlier. That conversation had haunted me, and now I couldn't get it out of my mind.

The second memory was more recent. During an exam in a class on teaching secondary English, our professor announced that he had graded the final papers we had written for the course, and in the pile was one that he considered the best student paper he had read in his twenty or so years as a college instructor. We all looked over at the guy we assumed had written the paper and then got back to our exams. As I turned in my exam, Dr. Styslinger stunned me by telling me that it was my paper he was talking about. He said I should seriously consider a career as a writer, that I had a feel for writing that he hadn't seen in a college student before. Once I came to my senses, I figured, *Right. He's just trying to steer me away from teaching because he knows I'll fail at that.*

I told one person, exactly one person, in that class what he'd said about my writing. She called me a liar. I could have used a little more validation than that. I couldn't prove my truthfulness by showing her what he'd written on my paper, because he had asked if he could hold on to it for a few more days. By the time he returned the paper to me, I decided I didn't like her anyway.

So as I read the ad for a proofreader at the *Asbury Park Press*, those two memories came together, and I had another what-the-heck moment. If it didn't work out, I could still try to get a teaching job, maybe in Uganda or someplace where there wasn't so much infighting.

Proofreading was the extent of my journalistic aspirations. I certainly couldn't be a reporter, and I doubted that anyone would consider me skilled enough to be an editor. Journalism still sounded so exotic to me, even after I started working in the production department and realized the newsroom crew was anything but exotic. Eccentric, yes; exotic, no.

As a proofreader, I had little interaction with the editors unless there was a problem. But one editor—I think he was the city editor at the time—found out that I was a college graduate and had majored in English. He started hanging around our area more than he needed to, but I didn't think much about it. That turned out to be a good thing, because all along he was gauging my suitability as a reporter, and if I had known that, I probably would have bolted. A few months later, I was hired as a reporter, and I was scared to death.

The only journalism course I had ever taken was a throwaway, a class that was required if I wanted to work on the yearbook in my senior year of high school. That's all we did the entire year. I learned nothing about journalism. Here I was, suddenly working in a highly competitive environment, without any specific journalistic skills or any idea what I was doing.

Though the *Asbury Park Press* had a name that sounded provincial, it was anything but. The paper was a powerful force in Central Jersey. It had the Asbury Park area sewn up, but it was in a hot contest with two rival papers for dominance in its northern and southern distribution areas. What's more, it was encroaching on the Trenton paper for the top spot in state coverage and on a North Jersey paper for coverage of the metro New York area. This was not the kind of place where you'd expect to find yourself working if you were a novice and a frightened one at that.

I felt like Moses. Not Moses as he came to be, but Moses as he was, a reluctant servant. *But God*, I argued, *I hate to ask people questions—how can I be a reporter?* I hadn't even been a communications major. Watergate had elevated the profession to a whole new level—or had caused it to sink to a whole new level, depending on your opinion of Nixon. Regardless, the power of the press could not be minimized; the persistence of a few reporters had been instrumental in bringing down a president and his administration. I was way out of my league. And yet I had been learning how to discern the will of God, and everything I knew about the way He acted in a person's life lined up to point me to this job. Still, I didn't fit in. Why He kept sticking my nose in places where I didn't belong was beyond me.

There was only one thing left to do. I had a real job and a real church, but it took all my energy to try to fit in to both environments. I needed a break, an opportunity to try my hand at something easy, something I knew I could succeed at.

It was time to get married.

CHAPTER 16

I hadn't planned on getting married so soon after college. And although I didn't really think marriage would be all that easy, I didn't expect it to be so completely miserable. The fact that I decided to go ahead and marry someone that I knew was all wrong for me might have played a tiny role in the failure of my dry run, the term I still use whenever I refer to that ill-fated, imperfect union.

ⓈⓈ ⓈⓈ ⓈⓈ

HE WAS A BARTENDER at the golf course restaurant, which should have been—and in truth was—my first clue that this would not work. My friends told me he was wrong for me. My family told me it would never work. His mother gave us five years, tops. My pastor refused to conduct the ceremony. His pastor—using that term is a bit of a stretch, I admit—was a bigoted, gruff man whose name I cannot even remember. About all I remember from the ceremony was standing at the altar, praying that this would work. I knew, as I stood there, that it would not.

Why did I marry him? Thirty years later, I'm still not sure. I wasn't even drinking at the time. I refuse to believe that it was because of his British accent and his sports car, though I admit they may have enhanced his appeal. I suspect I was simply in the mood to get married. I did go for counseling, and I did try to listen to everyone's objections. But in the end, my decision to get married came down to one night when I was alone with my Bible.

Maybe the Catholics knew what they were doing all those centuries when they kept the Bible out of the hands of common folk

like me. I once heard someone say that a little religion is a dangerous thing, and that proved to be the case for me that night. I had just
enough faith, and just enough understanding of how God works in
the lives of ordinary people, to ruin my life once again.

We were already well into our wedding plans when I conducted
this fateful little experiment in personal Bible study. I knew I should
break off the engagement, but in recent years, I had become so all-
fired committed to whatever I set out to do that breaking this commitment, this engagement, was incredibly difficult. What would my
fiancé think if I, a Christian, reneged on my promise to marry him?
What would his parents think? They weren't in favor of the wedding
anyway, so that was hardly a valid concern. If I really cared so much
about my witness as a Christian, the real question should have been:
What would they think if they knew I was going through with this
marriage even though I was convinced it was destined to fail?

Undeterred, I pulled out my trusty *Young's Concordance* and
looked up every variation of words like *marriage* and *betrothal* that I
could think of. I prayed first, of course, something like *God, I will
not get married unless You give me clear direction through a Bible
verse that I should go ahead with it.* Under my breath, I was saying,
"Yeah, sure, I know the verse about being unequally yoked, but let's
just forget about that one for now."

I spent several hours poring over verse after verse, trying to make
them fit my plan. Nothing worked. I was getting very discouraged,
especially because I was nearing the end of the Old Testament. I
knew full well what the New Testament had to say, and I decided I'd
rather not go there.

Finally, there it was, staring me in the face, the answer to all my
problems—Hosea 2:19, underlined to this day in my New American
Standard Bible: "And I will betroth you to Me forever; Yes, I will
betroth you to Me in righteousness and in justice, In lovingkindness
and in compassion, And I will betroth you to Me in faithfulness.

Then you will know the LORD." *That's it!* I thought. *I will marry him, and then he will come to know the Lord!* Of course, there was that pesky problem of the capitalized pronouns, meaning this had something to do with God getting married and not two mortals getting married, but that was easy enough to overlook.

So we got married, and I made every mistake in the book trying to keep the marriage intact. I tried with all my might to make those verses in Hosea come to pass, but my husband just wouldn't cooperate for some reason. We separated six months shy of our fifth anniversary, fulfilling not the words of Hosea but the prophecy uttered by my husband's mother.

☙☙ ☙☙ ☙☙

WHILE THIS ROMANTIC DRAMA was unfolding, I was working at the newspaper and feeling more out of place every day. Everyone there was so cynical, and I was still in my honeymoon phase with Jesus. Despite what was going on at home, there were days when I would walk into the newsroom so filled with spiritual joy that I could hardly contain it. During one particularly exhilarating period, I positively bubbled over with divine enthusiasm, drawing the wrath of a hardened, broken-down copy editor who made it known that he loathed the very sight of me. It's not as if I was evangelizing—I was just happy. This did not fit the image of a cynical reporter, the only kind of reporter that anyone respected, meaning I'd either have to lose the smile or risk being branded a lightweight. It took a few years, but eventually the cynicism won out.

There's probably no environment more rich in productive misfits than the newsroom of a daily newspaper. My faith set me apart, so I never really felt as if I fit in, but I came close. For one thing, the stereotype of the hard-drinking newsman, or newswoman, is no exaggeration. Granted, it may apply to a minority of the newsroom population, but it's a pretty accurate image, or at least it was back in the 1970s and 1980s. Although I didn't imbibe in my early years at the paper, I knew how to handle any co-worker who had partaken of a liquid lunch. On many occasions, I covered for them—not to keep management from knowing that the person had been drinking, because management always knew, but to keep the editors from humiliating the reporter. I'd clean up the copy of some inebriated reporter before he or she turned it in to the editor in charge. Of course, when it was an editor who was under the weather, things got a bit tricky. I'd head for the production department under some pretense or other, and there I'd make last-minute corrections to copy that had been "edited" and sent by a tipsy editor. I was glad to help out; it was my way of redeeming the years that I had spent totally sloshed. Management was there to handle the much larger problem of employee alcoholism.

There were a few pain-in-the-neck people on staff, and the last I heard, a couple of editors were still working there who swear that one incompetent reporter in particular made me so mad that I threw an ashtray across the room, even though I have no memory of such an ugly display of ill-bred character. But for the most part, my co-workers were talented and creative and just about the wittiest people I've ever known. A friend once described my sense of humor as wicked, and if that's what it is, I know exactly which group of people planted the seed and watered it and cultivated it and watched it grow to maturity.

Although I thoroughly enjoyed most of the people I worked with, my favorites were the genuine characters, the older reporters and editors. They were the ones who had paid their dues and come up through the ranks on the basis of their guts and talent and tenacity. Some of them looked as if they lived somewhere in the bowels of the building, having not seen a single ray of sunlight in decades. Others were just plain eccentric, like the reporter who was so fastidious that he could not abide the thought that someone on the night crew would be using his typewriter. Each day when he left, he would place a cover over his Remington, as if that would prevent a night-beat reporter from using it. Heaven help the reporter who did use it but failed to place the cover back on just so.

In contrast to these seasoned pros, most of the reporters who were my age had gone to J school, as journalism school had come to be known, and some had master's degrees in communications. They were the ones with more degrees than talent, who walked right in to the plush jobs. After I became an editor, I discovered that a few—including at least one Ivy League graduate—could not even write a coherent sentence, which is what precipitated the alleged ashtray-throwing incident that I continue to deny. If it did happen, and I'm not saying it did, my actions were justified, believe me.

Actually, I could have thrown all the ashtrays I wanted to without fear of reprisal, because I didn't care about progressing through the ranks or becoming anything more than the beat reporter I was. I had stumbled into this job, this career, and I didn't expect to ever advance beyond what I was, a municipal reporter covering borough council and school board and zoning board meetings in several towns and writing an occasional feature. But before my first anniversary at the paper rolled around, management offered me a promotion—to what one colleague called a dead-end position, the most thankless job in the whole building, lower than a janitor. I would be the religion editor.

CHAPTER 17

*M*y tenure as religion editor began in the summer of 1973, and most people who held that position lasted a year or two at most. It wasn't a full-time beat; I still had several municipalities to cover, and I was expected to fit the religion beat in wherever I could.

෧෨ ෧෨ ෧෨

MY TENURE LASTED TEN FULL YEARS. Only for my firstborn would I give up that thankless job.

Once I got my feet wet, I realized that the newspaper's poor excuse for a religion page would never do. What I inherited was a half-page church section that consisted mainly of a list of church services. Because it ran on Saturday, notices about Jewish services were either ignored or run a week early, as if anyone would leave the Saturday paper hanging around the house for a full week. So I got the page switched to Friday, and I asked for more space. There was so much going on in the religious world, and we were acting as if the only important thing was the bake sale at Holy Trinity. And that was another thing I changed right away; I got rid of announcements of any events that were not religious. Forget rummage sales, bake sales, bingo, potluck suppers—all of those notices went over to the social pages.

The guy who had done the page before me thought I was nuts. He had trouble filling half a page, and here I was asking for more space and getting rid of what had been the meat and potatoes of the section when he was in charge. I'm sure he wasn't alone in his assessment. Then there were those who feared that I would turn the section into a full-page ad for Jesus. Honestly, you commit your life to the Creator of the universe, spend every waking hour in fellowship with Him, and the next thing you know, people think you're a fanatic.

Despite my zeal, they needn't have worried. I knew the definition of *objective*, and I'm sure that came as a surprise to some of my detractors. When I started a series on the world's great religions, in which I offered a capsulized glance at the beliefs and geographical extent of the top twenty or so faiths and denominations, they pretty much shut up and found someone else to pick on.

Outside the newsroom, though, I faced my most vocal critics—Christians who wondered if I could truly be one of them and write all these stories about Muslims and Buddhists. The biggest outcry came after I wrote a feature on the Metropolitan Community Church, a gay denomination that had just set up shop in Asbury Park. You would think I had published an enrollment form and beckoned one and all to come join the gays in worship for all the flak I took over that one story.

And I attracted the loonies, the genuinely disturbed people who felt it their religious duty to keep me in line or convert me to their faith, which nearly always emanated from someone who claimed to be the Messiah.

I even had my own personal groupie, a guy named Lance who claimed to be in love with me. We had never met—at least not that I know of, a thought that still makes me shudder—and all his letters came to me from someplace in North Jersey. This long-distance stalker gave me the creeps, but he didn't do anything that I could take to the police.

That wasn't the case with another letter writer. He sent me typewritten, anonymous letters mailed from all over the tri-state area—New York, New Jersey, and Pennsylvania. Each had a particular identifying mark, and each carried a threatening tone. My managing editor and I decided just to keep the letters on file but be extra vigilant for any sign that he was about to do something other than write letters.

One day, a reporter at a newspaper near Philadelphia called me and wanted to know who I thought I was, sending this nasty letter to him. It turned out that the menacing letter writer had started writing to other religion editors and was signing my name to his missives. We called the postal service immediately, and they got the FBI involved. The letters stopped just as immediately, but it was a long time before I could walk down the street without feeling as if I was being watched.

Compared to Lance and the menace, others who tried to bedevil me proved to be ineffectual amateurs. Bona fide nutcases would write to me and sign their letters as Satan; one admirer warned me I was going to face the flames of hell because of a typo in a Scripture reference. "The Word of God cannot be changed!" he warned, so incensed that he must have temporarily forgotten that the Holy Spirit didn't exactly say, "OK, now Luke, the next verse will be numbered 5:10, and it will read . . ." I'm sure this particular fan was smart enough to realize that. Yes, I'm positive he was.

The fact that I survived all these misguided attempts to set me straight theologically has to be credited to the power of prayer. Not my prayers, but the prayers of the many people who asked God to protect me and guide me in my job. And no one was more faithful in praying for me than one group of Catholic priests and nuns. They were affiliated with the People of H.O.P.E., which stood for the House of Prayer Experience, and they were the first charismatics I ever met. Initially, my interest in the group was purely journalistic, but they were so friendly and so open and so hip that I would drop in to visit with them from time to time. These were not the Catholics of my childhood; these Catholics laughed and sang and chanted in the Spirit and placed my name on their daily prayer list, thanks to my strategic position on the newspaper. Because they were so cool, I had to respect what they were doing. But at first, I had no idea what they were doing, just that it sounded faintly wacko.

Like lots of kids who came into a life of faith through the Jesus People, I thought our experience with Jesus was unique. It was like the first time you fall in love, when you know with unshakable certainty that no one in the history of the world has ever felt what you feel. Others may have believed that they were in love, but you and you alone had chanced upon the real thing. No other couple's relationship could ever come close to what the two of you share.

That's the way we felt about Jesus. We thought we were the first generation to ever have such an exciting and intimate relationship with the Son of God. Anyone who had a life of faith apart from the Jesus People couldn't know what spiritual reality was. In our case, I can't say we were guilty of spiritual arrogance, especially after confronting genuine spiritual arrogance far too often since then. I think we were simply spiritually ignorant. Most of us had no knowledge of the rich historical writings of believers whose intimacy with Jesus was unparalleled, and we were too blinded by our own expression of faith to recognize the real thing in other people whose expression of faith differed from ours but was just as real.

It was with this attitude that I first approached the charismatic renewal in general and the People of H.O.P.E. in particular. The more time I spent with them, the more clearly I could see that they had something I wanted: a vibrant relationship with God that could be attained by exercising the gifts of the Spirit, and a deeper relationship with God that could be acquired through contemplative prayer. Only among Catholic charismatics did I find this convergence of two seemingly contradictory spiritual activities; in fact, only among those Catholics who had taken monastic vows did I think such a combination was possible. Surely you couldn't live a contemplative life outside a monastery. I envied the nuns who lived at the

H.O.P.E. house in Asbury Park. I longed for the simplicity of their lifestyle; their lack of attachment to material things fell into line with one of my most strongly held convictions, which just about everyone in the late 1970s considered to be a foolish by-product of the idealism of the counterculture. But here was a group of people living that way, the way I had always wanted to live. The only problem was that they were nuns, for goodness sake.

Their devotion to Jesus put mine to shame. More than any other group of believers at that time, the People of H.O.P.E. showed me that we in the Jesus People movement were not the sole curators of a living relationship with the Lord. They made their faith so appealing that I was just about ready to cash in my Protestant chips and became a latter-day Maria von Trapp, except that I couldn't sing and I was married, on paper anyway. Like the young Maria, I probably wouldn't have been an asset to the abbey, but at the time I was more concerned about what I could get rather than what I could give.

My visions of fleeing to a nunnery were mere flights of fancy, if for no other reason than the celibacy requirement. If not for that, I might have given the notion some serious thought, so attractive was the lifestyle to me.

Resigned to the fact that the contemplative, monastic life was not available to me, I turned instead to the other aspect of their lives, the part that had them speaking and singing and chanting in tongues. For a dyed-in-the-wool Baptist, this was at least as creepy as the graven images had been when I was a child.

But the charismatics I met managed to make all these unusual spiritual activities seem less creepy, and every time they pointed out their similarities to the first-century church, I'd get all tingly. Privately, I sensed the delicious thrill of spiritual rebellion once again. I knew it wouldn't be long before I traded in my fundamentalist card for a Holy Spirit encounter.

CHAPTER 18

B y the late 1970s, post-counterculture America was ready to get back to normal, which did not bode well for me. Women in particular were looking at me funny, and I got the sneaking suspicion that they were wondering if I were a female impersonator. We were so unisex during college and the '60s; both sexes wore bell-bottoms and sandals and beads, but now I was supposed to look and act like a respectable woman. I may have already been respectable, but appearances, as we know, are far more important than character.

☙☙ ☙☙ ☙☙

I WAS NOW DRESSING MODESTLY, which should have been enough. But it wasn't. There were all these rules about the kind of jewelry you should wear with certain outfits and the color of clothes you were allowed to wear before and after Labor Day and Memorial Day. It was all so confusing to one who considered denim to be an all-occasion fabric and color and didn't take kindly to nonsensical rules. On many of those all-occasions, I'd go ahead and wear whatever I wanted to, drawing more than the usual strange and disapproving looks.

If clothes had been the only problem, that would have been bad enough. But I did not act and think the way a typical young American woman was expected to act and think, which at the time would have been a cross between Mary Richards on the *Mary Tyler Moore Show* and Olympic figure skater Dorothy Hamill. So here I was, already a misfit, and I couldn't even fit in with my own gender. It wasn't as if I had some kind of gender identification problem. I was a woman through and through, just not the kind that society wanted me to be.

I considered bridal and baby showers to be the ultimate exercise in boredom and foolishness. I didn't even agree with the concept of a shower, let alone some of the activities that took place at these gatherings, like dressing the bride-to-be in a toilet-paper gown or adorning the mother-to-be with a paper-plate-and-bow bonnet. I was all for giving people stuff, especially first-time parents or young couples who had lived with their parents and needed so many big and little things to set up a house together. But most of the engaged couples I knew had lived on their own—or together—for years and had way too much stuff already.

Once I got engaged, I made it clear that I did not want a shower. I was so adamant about it that I even made my future mother-in-law cry. She apparently already had a surprise shower planned, though she knew I did not want any kind of shower. Of course, I had no knowledge of the surprise shower, and one day I made some offhand remark about how I thought the only thing worse than a bridal shower was a surprise bridal shower. She burst into tears, and I felt crummy when I found out why, but it didn't change my opinion in the slightest.

My sister, in typical big-sister fashion, ignored my wishes and sprang a small surprise shower on me. The photos from that auspicious occasion show me crying my eyes out, and I'm sure everyone thought I was shedding tears of joy and gratitude. But no, my sister had lured me to her apartment by telling me my brother and his wife had just arrived for a surprise visit with their newborn son, who was a month old at the time. That was so out of character for Thurman; he never did anything spontaneously, but I was so excited about seeing his baby that I wasn't thinking clearly.

When I got there and realized that my newborn nephew was nowhere within a hundred-mile radius of that apartment, I burst into tears. My negative opinion about surprise showers had just been irreversibly confirmed.

I also thought weddings, including my own, were a pain, though not so much the weddings of people I knew well and loved deeply. But it seemed as if every month I would get a wedding invitation from couples I hardly knew. I knew full well they didn't want me there to "celebrate their special day" with them; that was patently evident when I showed up for the service but declined to attend the reception. Somehow, even if I sent my regrets and a gift, my failure to make an appearance at the reception seriously offended the couple, who in some cases wouldn't have known me from Eve to begin with and wouldn't have liked me no matter what.

Then there were the product parties of the Tupperware type. I confess I did a brief stint with Shaklee, and that remains one of the most humiliating blots on my checkered past, even more humiliating than all the times I wore earrings that clashed with my outfits. Mainly, I just sold the Shaklee nutritional products to one person at a time, but occasionally I got roped in to hosting a skin care party.

And makeup—I could never quite get the hang of it. Foundation would often slide right off my face and onto my clothes, or else it would evaporate and disappear into the ozone layer, no doubt creating a hole for which I will someday be held accountable. After years of frustration, I've given up. I only wear makeup now under extreme duress, like when I feel compelled to celebrate the beginning of a new millennium or when otherwise nice people tell me they need that dreaded marketing tool, a publicity photo.

Whether I wear makeup or not, people have always told me I look tired. I could be as fresh as the proverbial daisy, ready to greet the day with renewed vigor and enthusiasm, and someone will invariably send me back to bed by saying something like, "Wow, are you feeling all right? You look really tired." I used to tell them I had inherited Edwards eyes, or more accurately, Edwards eye bags.

Because these days I generally wake up with a gallon of Folger's rather than renewed vigor and enthusiasm, I agree with those ever-observant commentators and start in with something like this: "Oh, I know. I must look absolutely exhausted. You can't imagine the night I had! First I tossed and turned until 2 A.M., and then—can you believe it?—I woke up again at 4 A.M. and . . ." By then, they've either realized how offensive their comment was or remembered a pressing appointment.

Why some women feel compelled to make daily, or hourly, comments on another woman's appearance is beyond me. Can you imagine men doing the same?

"Tony! What a nice tie you're wearing today."

"Thanks, Gary! But you're looking awfully tired! Are you all right?"

I used to work with a woman who commented on some aspect of my appearance—my clothes, my shoes, my hair, my makeup—every day, and she wasn't even the fashion editor. It got to the point where I'd scrupulously examine myself from top to bottom before I left the house each morning, trying to anticipate what exactly she'd single out. Her "compliments" were always so transparent: "Now, *that's* a nice dress"—implying that perhaps the one I wore the day before, or every dress I had worn in the past, didn't quite cut it. This woman happened to work at the newspaper, but her clones have been present at every other place where I've worked. Other women didn't seem to consider this kind of behavior peculiar; I was the peculiar one for thinking it a nuisance.

Every workplace seemed to have a resident diet expert as well. Few topics are as tiresome to me as food and diets and weight loss, and my inability to converse intelligently about these topics kept me out of the loop in the office, just as my refusal to talk about detergents kept me out of the loop in other groups. I'd be at someone's house for the Super Bowl or some big sports event, and the women would start talkin' Tide. My eyes would glaze over, and I'd sit there in a catatonic state, only realizing hours later that the women had retired to another room and I was alone in the TV room with their husbands. I was not a popular guest.

Thanksgiving always offered the greatest visible pulpit for my silent sermonizing. Because as soon as the meal was over, I'd head for the living room or the family room with the guys and the children, leaving the other women to clean up. I wasn't trying to get out of work; I was trying to make a point. But no one seemed to get it. I'd pontificate about how the women made the meal and the men ought to clean up, but the women never joined my strike, and the men never budged. I was understandably branded as an annoying feminist, though I didn't consider myself to be either one.

For one much too long period in my life, I was outspoken and tried to make a point about everything. I realize now that it was just my way of trying to explain myself; if I kept harping on these unpopular opinions I held, maybe people would either understand me better or even begin to agree with me. Then too, I may have been hoping that by drawing attention to the ways in which I differed from them, they would stop putting so much pressure on me to be something I was not, something I could never be. But it only served to alienate me from other women, and rightfully so.

I admit now that so many of the things I did were discourteous. I even went through a phase in which I refused to send thank-you notes, because I thought gift-givers went way overboard in their resentment toward anyone who didn't send a proper thank-you note. My warped thinking ran something like this: I never noticed if someone failed to thank me in writing, so why should anyone notice if I didn't send a note? And besides, why would anyone bother to give a gift if they didn't think the recipient appreciated it? I once received a totally blank thank-you note from a bride who obviously had way too much going on. From another bride, I received a short but gushing note thanking me for the wonderful wedding gift; the problem was, the customized gift I had ordered for her wasn't ready in time for the wedding, and I hadn't had a chance to give it to her yet. Both incidents underscored my opinion of how insane it is that we place these kinds of expectations on each other.

Over time, I figured out which female behaviors constituted the culture's idea of a minimum daily requirement. I was willing to adapt to a certain degree, but I was not willing to overdose.

CHAPTER 19

*M*aybe it was this whole problem I had trying to fit in as a woman that finally drove me from the Baptist Church. I'd look at the older women in the church, and they seemed so weighed down by the burden of being churchwomen. I don't know what ever possessed me to think that the situation would be any different in any other church. Maybe I was just ready for a change. And it only took three little words to get me to jump ship.

☙☙ ☙☙ ☙☙

THOSE WORDS—*PRAISE THE LORD!*—greeted me when I called a local United Methodist church to get some information for the religion page on a professional football player scheduled to speak at the church on the following Sunday. "Praise the Lord?" I hadn't heard anyone use that phrase in normal conversation since the heady days of the Jesus People. This was 1976, and the heated fervor of the Jesus People had cooled considerably. Furthermore, this was a Methodist church. John Wesley may have been quite the radical in his day, but since then, Methodists had generally sobered up, spiritually, that is. "Praise the Lord" might be heard in a hymn or two, but no respectable Methodist would actually talk that way.

The woman who answered the phone turned out to be respectable enough, though I guess not a respectable Methodist, because she and her husband later got the boot. But on the day I called, they were still the pastoral couple in charge of a small United Methodist flock at the Jersey Shore. I got the information I needed, heard "Praise the Lord" a few more times, and hung up determined to put all my investigative reporting skills to work. Which on the religion beat meant that I'd be going to church.

Under the guise of checking out this football player's conversion story, I slipped into an unoccupied pew a safe distance from the pulpit. The first time you go to a church, you never know whether you're committing some unholy breach of etiquette by having the unmitigated gall to sit in the Thompson family pew, the one the Thompsons had been sitting in for three generations, or the one dedicated to the memory of our dear sister Dorothy, but God help you if you sat there and hadn't known Dorothy before she went to be with our Lord.

Nobody shot me a nasty look, so I figured the pew was up for grabs. When my buddy Rusty—an old friend from the Ocean Front House and the Baptist church—walked in, I knew I was on solid ground, even if it was denominational ground. My only faux pas was to hug the woman in front of me when the official greeting time arrived—she was a coldhearted hand-shaker—but by then I was so overcome by all the hallelujahs and all the joyful faces that I forgot myself. As it turned out, the joyful faces were few and far between, but because I was sitting in an unclaimed back pew, I didn't know that. Some reporter I was—there was trouble afoot, and I didn't even see it coming.

Three months later, the pastoral couple was out the door. The stalwarts of the faith would have none of this "Praise the Lord!" and "Hallelujah!" stuff, plus there were rumors that the couple and their followers spoke in strange tongues. That threw me off a bit at first; I knew the People of H.O.P.E. spoke in tongues, but they were Catholic, and therefore strange. At least to me.

So this couple went off on their own—I mean, stepped out in faith—and started an independent charismatic church. I liked the word *independent* so much that I gave it a try. I stayed for eleven years.

Now if you weren't in a charismatic church in the late 1970s, or if you didn't read certain Christian magazines, then you probably never heard of the shepherding movement, also known as the discipleship movement, which stressed accountability to such a degree that in its worst manifestations, leaders exercised the right to determine things like who a man in the church should marry, which job he should take, and what kind of car he should drive. Married women were to submit to their husbands completely; single women were to submit to the female leaders of the church.

In the beginning, I hardly paid attention to the way this teaching was taking root in our church. My life was crumbling before my eyes; I had failed at marriage, the one and only thing I had assumed I could do right. The people at church kept me alive with their hugs and prayers and encouragement. With them, I could cry openly, something I had seldom done since I sobered up. Back in my drinking days, depending on the particular combination of adult beverages that I had imbibed, I'd cry at the least provocation. I remember sobbing at a bar one night—and singing "Reason to Believe" right out loud—all at the death of folksinger Tim Hardin. The problem was, that was in 1971, and Hardin didn't die until 1982.

My preoccupation with my divorce kept me blissfully unaware of the direction our church was heading. Occasionally, I'd be taken aside and chided for saying something out of turn, something that sounded as if I was undermining the authority of the pastor. I thought I was simply expressing my opinion, like the time I wondered out loud whether God really cared if we showed up for each and every meeting, which at one point was a requirement if we wanted to be considered members in good standing. I thought I was behaving by not asking whether God cared if we were members in good standing.

I knew rebellion inside and out, and I sure didn't think I was rebelling against anyone or anything. I loved that church and everyone in it, except for this one blowhard who always rubbed me the wrong way and ended up abandoning his wife and child for his secretary. You can't always tell what someone's up to, but with this guy, you just knew something was rotten somewhere. He once gave a teary-eyed testimony—this was before his little indiscretion became public—about how blessed he was to be able to take part in a certain ministry with his wife. I wanted so much to tell the pastor that I thought this guy was full of baloney and shouldn't be allowed any kind of public platform until he had proven himself, but I knew I'd seal my reputation as a rebel if I ever did anything that appeared to question my pastor's judgment. So I kept my mouth shut, and six months later, this guy was in divorce court, testifying to all manner of disgusting things about his wife. Even if the things he said were true, which they weren't, only a jerk would speak of them out loud and on public record, no less. I rest my case.

It was right about this time that one of my friends warned me that I was becoming a Stepford wife to this particular church. I objected, but I had no idea what she was talking about. I just knew it didn't sound good. The next time she repeated the accusation— she was determined to get her point across—I asked what a Stepford wife was. It seems there was this movie about a town called Stepford in which the husbands had replaced their wives with perfect little robotic servants; by comparison, June Cleaver and Donna Reed were downright scandalous in their rebellious ways.

The more she talked, the more I saw that in some ways, she was right. I didn't think I had succumbed to the kind of mind control she described, but then again, a person who is under the control of someone or something else seldom sees it or admits it. But I did agree that the church was exerting an enormous amount of pressure on the people in leadership, mainly the couples who led small groups in their homes. They were required to think and believe and even dress a certain way. There would be no individuality among the leaders. A tight chain of command ensured that any and all situations would be dealt with in a manner prescribed or approved from the top of the chain. Men who were in training to become deacons were admonished to keep their wives in line. If a married woman did not wholeheartedly agree with the church's practices and teachings, her husband was required to notify an elder, who would go to the couple's home and pray deliverance over the wife. Creative problem-solving didn't stand a chance. I watched perfectly normal people turn into a living, breathing cast of characters straight out of *Mr. Rogers' Neighborhood*. On that show, if King Friday said the sun was shining, well, then, the sun was shining, no matter how high the floodwaters reached.

Meanwhile, the leaders of the shepherding movement, some of whom have since publicly repented for the damage they did back then, got on this kick where they detected a Jezebel spirit in any woman who dared to open her mouth and express an opinion. The Jezebel of the Bible was a ruthless, idol-worshiping woman who would stop at nothing to get what she wanted, whether it was a piece of land or the death of the prophet Elijah. It was quite a leap from her to a friend of mine, who once tried to explain to our pastor's wife the seriousness of clinical depression. That night, an elder paid a call on my friend's husband and warned him that his wife had a Jezebel spirit.

For the longest time, I believed I was one of only a few women in the church that the leadership had considered a Jezebel. But no, it turned out that any thinking woman was a Jezebel; in fact, it seemed that any woman who was not in leadership was at some point branded a Jezebel. Eventually, the label was attached to anyone who disagreed with the church on even minor points. To this day, some twenty-five years later, I still occasionally hear from women from that church and other churches who were also told they had a Jezebel spirit. With so many of us running around, apparently intent on bringing down the church, you'd think we would have been a little more effective. As it is, the church is still going strong. But so are we, so I'm guessing they prayed that spirit right out of us when we weren't looking.

The sad thing is that I loved these people, and I couldn't understand how they could inflict this kind of damage on so many church members. They came between husbands and wives, promoting certain teachings as gospel—as if all couples were created equal. In a home in which the balance of responsibility did not compute to their liking, they'd draw the husband aside and give him a lecture on—what else?—Jezebel. It didn't matter that the couple might be happily married, respectful of each other's strengths and weaknesses. It didn't matter that they had created a beautifully functioning union; if it didn't function the way the leadership said it should, it couldn't be biblically correct. The pressure put on some of the men in the church was unimaginable; the blame leveled at some of the women was shameful.

I completely abandoned any Stepford tendency I might have had one Sunday when a man I'll call Jack, a wanna-be professional singer, came out on the stage to sing and profess his newfound love of Jesus. This man's wife was a good friend of mine, and I figured that if he'd had any kind of genuine conversion, I probably would have heard about it. I tried to give him the benefit of the doubt, but the longer he sang and testified, the sicker I got. It was happening again. The leaders were giving a public platform to someone who had not had time to become grounded in his faith, if he even had any faith at all.

I waited several weeks. I prayed. I checked my attitude to make sure I wasn't out of line. When I finally felt that the time was right, that my heart was right, that the atmospheric pressure was right, I decided to talk to my pastor. In the intervening weeks, I had even avoided Jack's wife so that my fondness for her would not influence me.

A person who has never been a part of a controlling church cannot imagine the mental and emotional gymnastics a person—most often a woman, in the case of this church—would go through before bringing a concern about anything in the church to the pastor or another leader. Most people just didn't bother. Maybe everyone else in the church knew Jack was a phony and knew better than to open their mouths about it. But years earlier, I had sat by and watched the blowhard devastate his family, and I believed way down deep that I had to bring my concerns to the pastor.

We met, and I told him that I sensed deep in my spirit that this guy was not for real. Even if he was, allowing him to join the worship team onstage seemed to be too much too soon, and I felt I needed to express my misgivings to him and the other leaders. He smiled and started telling me some story about how whenever a man started to assume the role of leader in his home, a little birdie would land on a woman's shoulder and whisper all kinds of things in her ear. I sat there totally confused, thinking he was talking about Jack's wife, even though that didn't make sense. I listened and tried to understand what he was saying, but I realized we weren't talking about Jack anymore. With a condescending smile, he as much as patted my head and said, "Run along, little girl, and let the big boys handle this." It wasn't until I got outside and started analyzing his story that I realized I was the woman with a little birdie on my shoulder, whispering in my ear, undermining the leadership team by questioning their ability to identify a true man of God.

I couldn't even feel smug when the wanna-be left his wife for another woman in the church some time later. This man had faked his conversion—not, by the way, a very difficult thing to do, if you're motivated enough—because he had a thing for this other woman.

Both she and her husband were believers and good friends with his wife. He was the odd man out; only by getting involved in the church could he gain this woman's trust. He did, and while her husband was away on a business trip, he came over to her house to offer the kind of help that only a man could provide. Two marriages were destroyed—three, if you count his subsequent marriage to the woman he pursued. She eventually left him for someone else.

The big boys handled it, all right. Sometimes, I guess, little birdies whisper the truth in your ear.

CHAPTER 20

So why didn't I leave this controlling church? For one thing, my relationship with God was relatively uncomplicated, and I didn't want to do anything to rock the boat. Every time I tried to leave, I would get this overwhelming sense that I should stay put. I tried praying about leaving, and I tried not praying about leaving. I would occasionally attend another church, but I never felt the freedom to leave my own church for good. As far as I was concerned, when things were going well between God and me, I could put up with all manner of abuse from other quarters.

෧ඁ ෧ඁ ෧ඁ

BESIDES, I WAS SERIOUSLY DISTRACTED. Even though my first marriage had ended so miserably, I knew that I was not cut out for the single life. But I also knew that if I ever married again, I was not going to settle for anything less than the kindest man on the planet. Kindness is not a quality that I would have given a whole lot of thought to had I not reviewed Anita Bryant's autobiography for the newspaper's book section. During a particularly stormy period in her marriage, she caustically asked her husband what he wanted from her. "Kindness, Anita," he said. The moment I read that, I knew that of all the things my first marriage lacked, kindness topped the list.

Granted, expecting the kindest man on the planet to wander into my life was not what you'd call a reasonable expectation. But wander in he did. There he was, John Ford, Webster's living definition of kindness, living only a few miles away from me. What are the chances?

I've never asked John what he was looking for in a wife, but my best guess is that he must have thought he needed a woman who would test his patience to the max. He's every bit the misfit I am, but he's a whole lot more tolerant of my misfit ways than I am of his. We've known each other since 1979, and in all those years, he's never said an unkind word to me. It helps that he doesn't ever say much of anything, but still, that's quite a record, and it's one that I love to tell people about. It puts the pressure on him to keep the streak going.

Back in 1979, of course, I just had to trust my instincts, which apparently had become more trustworthy. John and I met right around the time my divorce had become final. We both knew I needed time, and a lot of it, to regroup and put my life back together again.

And once again, I needed to sober up.

෬෬ ෬෬ ෬෬

YOU'D THINK THAT GIVEN MY INTIMATE historical relationship with alcohol, I would know better than to believe I could ever safely have another drink. And you'd be right, of course—I did know better. But safety wasn't my primary concern the summer I turned thirty; with all those '60s rallying cries—like "Never trust anyone over thirty"— still floating around in my countercultured mind, I was about to join the ranks of Those Who Can Never Be Trusted. And I didn't like it one bit.

Still, I hadn't planned to mark the occasion with a toast. After my first marriage had ended, I had taken to drinking again, this time with my newspaper friends. But by the time my thirtieth birthday came around, I had been sober for quite a while. My close friends knew not to suggest we go out and celebrate. Even my former drinking buddies at the newspaper made sure I ordered a Tab when we went out for lunch on my birthday. But I hadn't counted on Scott, as

I'll call him, my neighbor, friend, and brother in Christ, to derail the festivities that so far had been dry.

More than anything, Scott wanted to honor me with a special dinner. A culinary school graduate who worked at a local restaurant, Scott could cook like there was no tomorrow. But he was also grossly underpaid, so my birthday dinner party consisted of Scott and me. This bothered him, especially because he figured I would want John to be there, but it didn't bother me at all. I was quite happy knowing I wouldn't have to relate to more than one person. The fewer, the merrier.

As soon as I arrived at his apartment, Scott—an upbeat guy even at the worst of times, the kind who would always laugh when he cried—began apologizing over this and that, how he couldn't find the proper ingredients at the stores around here, so the fish didn't turn out right, and was it too hot in here? And he had really wanted everything to be perfect for me, but . . .

I tried to assure him that everything was just fine, that I was thrilled at the obvious effort he had made to please me, that he was the best chef on earth, and all that. He relaxed a bit and suddenly remembered something that brightened his entire demeanor: the bottle of Pouilly-Fuissé chilling in the refrigerator. God bless him, he had remembered; I loved Pouilly-Fuissé.

"Scott, I can't drink." I acted as if I meant it, but it sounded pretty lame, even to me.

"I know, but it's your birthday. Just have a sip. Here, I'll pour just a little." True to his word, Scott poured probably no more than three ounces in my glass. As he raised his glass for the obligatory birthday toast, I looked into the shining eyes of a fellow misfit—and took what I knew to be a potentially deadly sip of wine.

At that moment, I didn't care. I had seen the pain and tears in Scott's eyes earlier that same year when his one trusted friend at church had "outed" him. Scott was gay, and even though he had avoided sexual contact since becoming a Christian, he knew he couldn't predict how the church would treat him if they found out about his past. But he needed someone to confide in, just one person he could talk to and pray with and call when he faced temptation. He chose carefully, he thought. But it turned out that his confidant "didn't know how to pray for him," so he told his wife what Scott had shared with him in private. No one knows exactly how it happened, but soon the whole church was aware of Scott's "problem."

So here I was, sitting in Scott's kitchen, turning thirty and getting madder by the minute at the thought of how he had been wronged. After all, I reasoned, any information about Scott's life was his to share, his and his alone. I worked myself into such a righteous snit that I bloody well took another sip. I finished the wine and felt much better.

Buoyed by my obvious victory over demon alcohol that night, I decided I was perfectly capable of having a glass of wine the following day. In fact, so decisive had been my victory that I marked the occasion with a second glass.

Six weeks later, the phone rang. A lot of things had happened between that second glass of wine and the phone ringing, but you couldn't prove it by me. I have no memory of those forty-plus days, and there are plenty of witnesses who could testify that there's a good reason for that.

I do remember answering that particular call. Because on the other end was Eileen, and when Eileen calls, you always remember it. There's not a whole lot that she lets you forget.

Eileen and I had made plans to pray together that night, that much I knew. Now I was doing my not-so-level best to worm my way out of it. All I wanted to do was go to bed and sleep it off, whatever "it" was that day. Bloody Marys, most likely.

One thing you need to know about Eileen: She doesn't take no for an answer. And another thing: She always, always puts her verbs at the beginning of a sentence. With Eileen, you experience conversation by command: Do this, pray that, go here, go there. I would even salute her on occasion.

So there I was, inebriated to the very core of my being, and I hear Eileen saying things like "Get over here now." I never knew anyone who could express a single thought in so many different ways, but then again, I never knew anyone like Eileen.

I got over there, now. And I sat in the corridorlike space that passed for Eileen's living room, feeling the walls close in on me even more and hearing Eileen blast me from there to kingdom come and back. For two full hours. With love in her voice. No one can yell at you so lovingly as this woman can.

After a while, I had apparently sobered up to her satisfaction, because she suddenly got really, really quiet. In fact, silent. She just stared at me for what felt like a day or two.

"Give it up."

"What?"

"Give it up. Tell God you'll never have another drink again. Make that vow to Him right now." Eileen would not know what to do with a verb if she couldn't put it in first place.

"Well, what if I have food that's made with wine and I didn't know it?" Thirty years old and trying to pull a grade-school tactic on a woman who practically invented the gift of discernment.

As expected, she discerned her way right through me. "Give it up."

And so, suddenly remembering the sobering fact that Eileen never takes no for an answer, I gave it up. Just like that.

I told God that I would never have another drink. I made a vow to Him right then. I meant it, and it didn't sound lame.

And then I prayed like there was no tomorrow.

☙ ☙ ☙ ☙

As I WAS SOON TO FIND OUT, there would be no tomorrow for some of the people in my life that summer, the summer of 1980, the year I sobered up for good. Within the next four years, AIDS would come to town with such a vengeance that it would manage to shake up the seemingly unshakable, the gay men and women who had defiantly emerged from their closets during the '70s.

The party was over for me, and for them, it soon would be.

Several gay men had provided a lifeline for me after my first husband left me. They liked to do the things I enjoyed—going to Broadway shows and museums and nice restaurants, or just hanging out in New York—all without the pressure of dating, which I had always hated. Then too, I was something of a decoy for a few men who were still afraid to let too many people know about their sexual orientation; being seen with a woman made them appear "normal," even if the woman at their side wasn't.

The weird thing is that I am hetero to the max: I cannot, for the life of me, understand same-sex attraction. I would spend time with these guys, but I would block out any thoughts about what they did that made them gay. I mean, I understood basic biology, but I wasn't interested in visualizing the variations.

I had long wondered why on earth God had brought so many gays into my life. Yes, I was more inclined to accept them than were most Christians I knew, and I wasn't embarrassed or afraid or horrified to be seen with gay men. They were outcasts, and I could certainly identify with that. But still, it did seem odd. Why so many?

By the time the medical community figured out what was killing so many Africans, Haitians, and gay men, John and I had married— three years to the day after we met—and a year later, I was pregnant with our first child. By then, I had lost contact with most of my gay friends, but the news began to filter back to me: A guy I knew in passing had died; several others were infected, but most had simply dropped out of sight, having crawled back into their closets to once again hide from an increasingly terrified heterosexual public. A terrified public that now included me: When our daughter Elizabeth was born in 1983, we already knew that this fatal disease was carried through the blood, and I had needed a transfusion following her delivery by caesarean section.

Once again, I found myself praying like crazy, this time over every drop of blood that entered my body. Though I appeared healthy over the following months, the terror would frequently return, like when the hospital where she was born discovered that some of the blood they had used in the fall of 1983—Elizabeth was born in October—was tainted with the virus that caused AIDS. Those who were infected would be notified, the newspaper story said. I was not among them, but for months I lived in dread that I would be called.

Even before the transfusion, I had glimpsed one of the reasons why God had brought so many gays into my life: to show them the unconditional love of Christ. If I hadn't done anything else, I knew I had done that. Every one of the gay men I knew was well aware of my faith in Christ. Now I understood the urgency behind all those friendships I'd had in the late 1970s, at a time when so many in the church had turned their backs on the homosexual community. I could only hope and pray that they would remember the things I had shared with them about Christ—and that they would see that there were those in the faith community who would not turn their backs on them now.

One of those was Eileen. Even if she had been straight, you'd peg her for the kind of Christian who would always embrace society's outcasts. But Eileen wasn't straight, or at least she hadn't been in recent years. She was the divorced biological mother of a teenage girl, and few people suspected her lesbian past. I sure didn't, and here I was surrounded by gay men.

We had been friends for probably a year before Eileen started telling me this story that seemed to go on forever.

She was sitting in a chair in the turreted section of my living room. At the time—1980, once again—I was renting the second floor of an old Victorian house owned by a couple named Heineken. I swear, that was their name. It was also the name of my favorite imported beer, but that really wasn't the main reason I rented the place. I loved the apartment, with its stained-glass windows and nineteenth-century character. So what if it overlooked a murky, trash-filled "lake" and the loading dock of Newberry's discount store just beyond? The house was in Ocean Grove, and the newsroom of the *Asbury Park Press* was just across the footbridge a block away.

Anyway, there was Eileen, who just a few months earlier had rescued me from a lifetime of bondage to alcohol, sitting in my living room and telling me all about some relationship she'd had with "this person." After a while—it *was* a long story—I felt like shouting, "All right already, I know 'this person' is a guy. Just say 'he,' OK?" It's a good thing I didn't, because Eileen started using the pronoun *she.*

That's what her long, rambling story was about: With more than a little discomfort, Eileen was trying to tell me about her lesbian past, and there I was trying to rush her along. So much for whatever pride I felt at being so sensitive to gays.

I'm sure I tried to hide my shock. After all, Eileen was one of my closest friends at the time, and although I knew she was different, I didn't know how different. But now I understood. Her particular weakness was among the more difficult to overcome; she had been a misfit even among misfits. But she had turned her life around and was no longer sexually active or a part of the homosexual community. Through this experience, she had learned firsthand about the transforming power of Jesus; her incisive understanding of human nature in turn transformed the lessons she learned into an exceptional ability to help other people apply scriptural principles to their own lives. That alone explained why so many outcast women looked to her for counsel.

But it was years before I realized why women like me tended to gravitate toward Eileen: There was a limit to what she would do to fit in. In Eileen, I found a woman who was comfortable with who she was—her past, her personality, her relationship with God and with the church. Although I had often balked at compromising my convictions in order to feel accepted by society and the church, I had a long way to go before I could say I had embraced my misfit-tedness as thoroughly and effortlessly as Eileen had embraced hers. Through my friendship with her, and a women's group ministry that we led together, I was learning to recognize the myriad ways that misfit women tried to fit in—and the damage those attempts inflicted on them.

Other women—at this time, mainly new believers who attended our women's Bible study—relied on Eileen to help them sort out who they were as new creations in Christ. On the one hand, the church was telling them about the unconditional love of Christ; on the other hand, the church was placing conditions on them. They were understandably confused. They had opened their lives to Christ by being vulnerable and transparent, exposing their true selves to Him and seeking His forgiveness. And they had received it. But now, the church let it be known that if they wanted to continue to be able to approach Christ—and fit in to the milieu of the church—they had to make some adjustments. They would have to jump through any number of hoops to feel as if they really belonged. Those hoops governed a range of religious activities, like tithing and daily prayer and Bible reading, as well as lifestyle issues, like cloth-ing style and leisure pursuits and parenting methods.

All too often, women would come to Eileen after the damage had been done. Some were in danger of losing their faith altogether.

The freedom they had found in Christ had quickly evaporated, as they found themselves trying to rearrange their lives, their families, and their personalities to conform to the church. In Eileen, they found someone who had managed to retain her individuality without leaving the church or walking away from God. So had I. But as determined as I was not to sacrifice my true self—the person Jesus loved unconditionally—on the altar of the church, it would take years before I put into practice what Eileen had already learned to do: Befriend her uniqueness instead of fighting it.

CHAPTER 21

*M*y mother-in-law—the real one, the one who gave birth to the kindest man on the planet—once warned me to be prepared for the day when I would not remember anything from my thirties. Surely, I thought, she was wrong about that. When she was in her thirties, she had four—four!—sons to distract her, and I didn't even have my first child until I was thirty-three. But she was right. That decade of my life is less clear than any other, though I doubt that has much to do with how busy I was. Instead, I'm fairly convinced that the spiritual oppression I was under led to an unhealthy degree of introspection which in turn muddied my everyday existence.

ල ල ල ල

THEN TOO, MY WORLD WAS SLOWLY starting to narrow down to my family. With Elizabeth's birth in 1983, I had left my job at the newspaper. Over time, I no longer socialized with anyone there.

But I was happy—and completely oblivious to the fact that someday, I would have to come to terms with the underlying issues that had once lured me toward addiction and now drew me toward isolation. Because I could claim victory over alcohol and drugs, because my attempts at fitting in certainly hadn't inflicted any damage on me, I thought the battle was over. Little did I suspect that my greatest battle was yet to come. An even stronger tendency—the habit of denial—would delay that battle for another ten years, but the problem brewed just under the surface of my life.

In the meantime, motherhood consumed me. The first complete, declarative sentence that I uttered after Elizabeth was born expressed my joy: "I want a dozen more children." John wrongly figured I would change my mind once the anesthesia wore off.

Now I was certain I had found what I was put on earth to do. Forget about becoming a nomadic professor or a teacher in Uganda or a newspaper editor or a door-to-door evangelist. I was cut out to be a mother, and I was going to be the best one ever.

Because most of my friends worked, I started hanging out with other stay-at-home mothers of young children. Once again, the blissfulness of my new life had blurred my vision. I joined La Leche, the breastfeeding group; I joined a mother-baby exercise class; I joined a parent-infant swimming class; I joined Elizabeth to me at the hip. All that would have been fine if it hadn't been for the compulsion we mothers felt about talking to each other. Really, if we had never struck up a conversation, who knows how long I could have continued the charade that I was normal? But that was not to be. We'd start talking about, say, breastfeeding, and I would start expressing my opinion that women should be allowed to breastfeed whenever and wherever they needed to as long as they were discreet, and that would end the conversation. So I would become the outcast breastfeeding mother among a group of breastfeeding mothers. I started to believe that never in my life had I held what could be called a popular opinion.

Then there was the matter of my age. Most of the mothers were in their early twenties, and to them, I was ancient. Eventually, my vision cleared enough to enable me to see that they were looking at me funny and probably had been all along. The clincher came when someone asked if Elizabeth was my granddaughter. I backed out of just about every group I had joined; I clearly did not fit in, even when I kept my mouth shut and my opinions to myself.

To make sure that my baby and I remained joined at the hip, I took leave of my senses and volunteered to run the nursery at church, which meant that I missed nearly every service for several years. That shouldn't have happened, because we used a rotating schedule of volunteer workers. But each week, it seemed, at least one assigned worker wouldn't be able to make it to church, so I would end up working. One Sunday, I managed to find a volunteer to cover for me, and I headed for the sanctuary for my first service in almost a year. A greeter welcomed me and handed me a visitor's packet; I was startled into realizing how long it had been since I had participated in anything resembling adult worship. After seven years as a member of the church, I was understandably treated like an outsider. There were so many new faces there that I felt as if I had walked into the wrong building.

Things were not exactly going my way. To make matters worse, any hope I had of having a large family was evaporating with each passing month. At first, I figured I wasn't conceiving because I was still breastfeeding. But even after I quit, I couldn't get pregnant.

Meanwhile, my father had died before John and I married, and my mother died shortly after Elizabeth's birth. We thought she'd lost her mind several years earlier when, at age seventy, she decided to drive from New Jersey to Alabama, by herself, to look up an old friend. But no. She was simply tough and determined. She held on to her mind a lot longer, losing it only when she lost her will to live.

No misfit friends, no adult fellowship, no parents, no suckling infant at my breast to pick up where Elizabeth left off. This could only mean one thing: God did not love me anymore.

If that seems like a stretch, trust me, it wasn't, considering the spiritual environment I was living in. The conventional theological wisdom in that environment went something like this: If you were healthy and wealthy, it was because God loved you and had poured out His blessing on your life. If you weren't healthy and wealthy, there must be some sin in your life. Because I couldn't conceive, I figured that qualified me as unhealthy, and since I had left work when Elizabeth was born, we sure weren't wealthy.

Sin was in the Ford camp, no doubt about it. Being well schooled in logic, I deduced that if God loved those He poured out His blessing on, then He must not love those He withheld His blessing from.

For the first time in my life, though, I had a scapegoat—John. He had to be the culprit. He must have had some hidden, unresolved sin in his life. I had seldom met anyone so kind and good-natured, and I figured there had to be something in his past that was coming back to haunt us. Try as I might, though, I couldn't convince God to have it out with John. With all the resources of the universe at His command, God could have produced any number of witnesses to some sordid incident in John's past that he had never dealt with. But John turned out to be a WYSIWYG kind of guy: What you see is what you get. He had no deep dark secrets in his past, and he was not the culprit. God seemed determined to make me sweat this out alone.

Considering all the references to sin in the Bible, it's no wonder that the topic had become a major focus of attention at church. Over the years, I've heard more bizarre teachings about the topic of sin than just about any other topic, except Jezebel, of course. I once heard a women's group leader tell a new convert that if you died with any unconfessed sin in your life, you'd go straight to hell.

This newly saved young girl asked in astonishment, "Do you mean that if I have a sinful thought and a second later I'm in a fatal crash, I'll go to hell?"

Without hesitation, the leader—handpicked by the pastor and charged with the responsibility of adhering to his doctrinal stance—answered, "Yes, that's right." This was at a time when no one dared contradict anyone in authority, and no one—myself included—spoke up. I was still smarting from my last talking-to, and besides, I could tell that the girl just wasn't buying it. I had to keep quiet and believe that God would straighten her out later.

Today, I wonder how I could ever have endured that kind of false teaching for as long as I did, especially considering that I knew it to be false. But it's not as if I woke up one morning and decided I would go out and find myself a nice controlling church to hook up with. And it's not as if the leaders of the church set out to create a controlling church. By his own admission, my pastor was far too trusting of other leaders who professed to be Christians. And he had placed himself under the authority of one of the now-infamous Fort Lauderdale Five, the group of national leaders responsible for the shepherding movement and its abuses—Don Basham, Ern Baxter, Bob Mumford, Derek Prince, and Charles Simpson. My pastor himself was under the control of a controller.

Like wolves in sheep's clothing, the false teachings and those who taught them gave the appearance of being doctrinally safe and sound. One of the first ideas that was introduced was the concept of covenantal relationship, the notion that we as a body of believers were in covenant with each other and with God, and we would stick together no matter how many demons came against us. Sounds great, until you realize the implications. The covenant relationship became foundational to all subsequent teachings, and because we were in covenant, we were expected to adhere to all these other teachings as well.

Like positive confession. What started out as a good idea—that you should be careful about what you say—turned quickly into superstition. There were all these people frightened to death that they would say the wrong thing out loud; I was once taken to task for admitting, right out loud, that I had a cold. Didn't I know that could give other people the impression that they could admit they had colds as well? Then where would we be? Everyone in the church would be sick!

The flip side of that was the magical use of positive confession. Would you like a bigger and better house? Then speak your desire, and—for some reason I still don't understand—God will be required to grant your wish. I thought my childhood image of God, this all-powerful being who cut down my grandparents to punish me for not getting baptized in time, was bad. But at least I never imagined Him to be a genie outside a bottle.

I regarded all of this as just so much silliness at the time, but in reality, it was serious business. Although the leaders were so ready to pounce on the likes of me for saying I had a cold, no one in authority in any charismatic church I ever attended seemed compelled to correct a heretical or false teaching. In one church, a visiting evangelist came right out and said that if you did not pray in tongues every day, you were living in sin. I knew the pastor and his wife did not believe that. They just sat quietly and let him continue his rant, but I was certain they would say something after he left or at the next service. They never said a word about it.

One of the most prominent beliefs among charismatics around the mid-1980s centered on the identification of whatever demon or demons were dominating a particular city or region. The last I knew, the practice of regularly praying against these demons by name had persisted. I don't know, maybe these demons do exist. People I greatly respect claim to have seen them and claim that the names of the demons had been revealed to them.

The true danger, though, seemed to be caused not by the demons but by the church leaders who coupled this teaching with the concept of "sin in the camp." If even one person in the church had sin in his or her life, the teaching went, then that person's sin would block the prayers of others who were intent on bringing down the city's demon. Women with particularly fragile and sensitive spirits began obsessively scrutinizing their lives to see if they could detect any hidden sin, and it became frightening to witness the outcome. One such woman in our church completely lost touch with reality and has never recovered mentally or spiritually.

Charismatics do seem to love absolutes. There are few gray areas in many of the teachings that some prominent charismatic leaders espouse. For one, there's the teaching that you must never touch "God's anointed"—meaning that you must never question the teachings or integrity or motivation of the leader who happens to be preaching at the moment. Those who champion that view conveniently ignore the context of the Bible verse that they use to support their position, Psalm 105:15: "Do not touch my anointed ones; do my prophets no harm." The verse refers to the kings of Israel as the anointed ones, and I haven't seen any of those lately. Even the reference to the prophets fails to apply to this misguided teaching, because the verse is prohibiting bodily harm; I know a few people who would like to remove that prohibition, but that's another story altogether. Finally, there's perhaps the most obvious question: If the anointed ones aren't the kings of Israel, then who are they? From what I can gather, the current thinking is that if a leader says he's an anointed one, then he's an anointed one. And if you can't touch his teachings, then you can't challenge his anointing. You get the picture.

I thought—hoped—that I had left the "God will strike you dead" mentality when I graduated from childhood, but some leaders have been so convincing in perpetuating this belief that there are grown-ups out there who actually live in the constant fear that they will collapse and die on the spot if they dare suggest that the leaders are in error. I half expect that some church will come up with a new anti-'60s bumper sticker: Never Question Authority. But I wouldn't want to give anyone a marketing idea like that.

Most harmful of all for me was the church's elitism, the unspoken implication that this church was the only one that offered love and acceptance and a fresh word from God. Each time I began to feel as if I was the only one who saw my beloved church crumbling before my very eyes, I would get the urge to bolt. But I would end up with the same conclusion each time: *Where else can I go? There's no other church that has what we have.* Years after I finally left the church, I realized how many times I had heard others in the church voice that same sentiment—and how cultlike it sounded.

We never did figure out which particular sin was plaguing the Ford camp. In mid-1987, four years after Elizabeth was born—and after spending the last two of those years crying and soul-searching and wondering why God had abandoned me—I discovered I was pregnant. I was so happy that I forgot to worry about the fact that God could still get me, if He wanted to, through miscarriage or stillbirth. I guess we had been good little Christians, because our second child, Sarah, was just as wonderful as Elizabeth was.

So there we were, healthy and happy but still not wealthy. That was unacceptable at our church, which had by that time taken on a country club aura. The leadership went after moneyed converts so we could move out of our rented facilities and build our own church; to their credit, the leaders openly said that was what they intended to do. They got their patron saints, and I began to feel like a poor relation once again. Then too, it was getting to be much too expensive to live in New Jersey. Real estate prices had skyrocketed, and John and I started talking about selling our house, which we had bought just two years earlier. We figured—correctly, as it turned out—that we could sell it for more than twice what we had paid for it.

Still, we had other considerations—his family, our friends, and our church. It took an act of faith, and my pastor's total misreading of that act, to convince me that it was time to go.

I had tithed religiously; even when times were tough, I would do my best to continue to give ten percent of our income to the church. One week, we had more than a thousand dollars in bills and $68.73 in the bank. I looked at that pitiful amount, looked at the bills that were due, and decided to give it all to God. I wrote out a check to the church, not to God, for exactly $68.73, leaving a zero balance. At the Sunday service a week after I had placed the check in the collection plate, my pastor gave us a talking-to about how stingy some of us are with God. "We're so precise with our tithe," he said in as sarcastic a tone as I had ever heard him use. "We get down to the penny with God and give Him some ridiculous amount like $68.73." Good grief! He thought that was my tithe? That was my all! I wish we had received $687.30 that week!

Instead of graciously accepting the check or at least giving me the benefit of the doubt, he chose to think the worst about me, that I was shortchanging God. That went a long way toward helping me make up my mind about moving. Our true friends would continue to be our friends no matter where we went. With my parents gone since the early '80s and the death of John's mother in 1989, there wasn't enough family left to prevent us from moving.

And clearly, we no longer had a church. As far as I was concerned, the covenant had been broken.

CHAPTER 22

*B*lessed with a significant enough gain on the sale of our house, we were free to move. We wanted to go someplace where real estate prices were still reasonable, but our main deciding factor was familiarity. We were uprooting our children, and to make it easier especially on Elizabeth, who was six, we thought we should relocate to an area where we already had friends or family, or to an area that we knew well. That narrowed our choices considerably: the Oregon coastline, where John's brother lived; the Shenandoah Valley of Virginia, where Merta now lived; or rural southern Delaware. Given that same roster of options today, I would choose Oregon in a heartbeat. Then and now, the Shenandoah Valley, as beautiful as it is, would fall to last place. Development had stripped the area of much of its charm, and housing prices were getting out of line.

有有 有有 有有

BUT RURAL SOUTHERN DELAWARE? Who besides the people who live there even know that the area exists? To me, the entire state of Delaware consisted of a fifteen-minute drive on I-95. The assistant pastor of our church in New Jersey, the church that had broken the covenant with us, had moved to Laurel, Delaware, several years earlier along with two other families. We counted all three families among our friends, so we headed south to an area populated by far more chickens than people. But after New Jersey, southern Delaware looked positively lovely. We had adapted to the sulfuric smell of New Jersey; we could adapt to the chicken-manure smell of Delaware.

Our five years in Delaware were far from perfect, but they were the most stable as far as our family life was concerned. I home-schooled the kids; John continued to work in inventory control, now for USAir; and we became involved in the church that Randy, our former assistant pastor, had started. It was fitting that we ended up there; Randy had married us, and we had missed him and his family after they left New Jersey. The church in Delaware was ideally suited to the needs of the people in the area. It was informal and relaxed and not at all flaky. Rural folks don't take kindly to flakiness.

For once, I felt as if I fit in with the dominant culture. Rural people for the most part are unpretentious and solid and, well, earthy. And they don't much care what other people think of them, providing valuable role modeling for me. We joined a home-schooling group where I found like-minded mothers who didn't mind that I was nearing forty and therefore borderline elderly.

Everything was going so well that you just knew the bottom was going to fall out. And it did. Randy, ever the restless one, had been offered a position in the suburban Chicago area. He and his family left, leaving behind the church and a big gaping hole in our lives. But we still had our home group, one of a number of small fellowship groups that met on Wednesday nights in members' homes, and soon, that group became our substitute for church.

Meanwhile, the congregation was going through a succession of interim pastors, one of whom decided to visit each of the home groups affiliated with the church. He visited ours, listened politely as one of the members gave a teaching, and finally said, "I've heard so many good things about you all, and you have a good group going here, but I never see you in church." Several of us burst out laughing; we realized how we must have come across to this poor guy who was trying to put a fragmented church back together again. And then we admitted that none of us really liked church very much, no matter who was in charge. Saying that right out loud marked a milestone for us, and hearing it probably did the same for him. For whatever reason, he did not become the permanent pastor. I'm not suggesting that we had a part in his decision, but there is that possibility.

Eventually, the congregation found a permanent pastor, and one of the first things he did was eliminate home groups. Our group kept right on meeting, of course, but after a while, we realized we had to make a choice. None of us had time to devote to two sets of meetings. As a substitute for home groups, the new pastor had started a small midweek meeting at a member's house. It wasn't anything like the home groups I had known; they had been warm and intimate groups of people who trusted each other and shared their lives with each other. This new version was completely different. We would sit and listen to another sermon, pray for a while, maybe sing a little, and then go home.

As I began to expect less from church, I began to expect more from God. It didn't occur to me what this actually meant, that I had been substituting church for God. All I knew was that I felt as if I needed something more from Him. I did my own version of "carpet time," charismatic jargon for falling under the power of the Holy Spirit. My carpet time was spent lying facedown on our bedroom floor, waiting and waiting and waiting on God. But, as songwriter Rich Mullins so precisely expressed it, God seemed to be playing hard to get.

Nearly every week, something would happen that would get my hopes up. Like the time the new pastor, Tom, asked me to stay for a while after one of those midweek meetings. From some of the conversation during the meeting, I gathered that one of the couples in the church needed immediate prayer and counseling. Finally, I thought, Tom has something for me to do. Maybe it's because I've been through a divorce, and he wants me to talk to the wife. Or maybe he has a word from God for me. I was so hungry, so desperate, so needy that I would have welcomed open rebuke, a harsh prophetic word, a spiritual spanking, anything.

Tom and his wife led the troubled couple to a back room where they prayed and shouted at demons and did all kinds of loud charismatic stuff as I sat on a stool at the kitchen counter. Tom's children were roughhousing in the living room, but I was too expectant, too eager for this word, this assignment from God, to give them much thought. As far as I could tell, they weren't being destructive, just being loud and rambunctious, typical for overtired young children after a long day and night. Eventually, the two couples emerged, and I prepared myself for whatever Tom had to say to me.

When the other couple left, I deduced that whatever Tom had to talk to me about, it must not have had anything to do with the couple's marital problems. I braced myself for whatever God had for me. I waited, awkwardly. Nothing. Finally I asked: "What did you want to talk to me about?"

"What?" Tom asked. "Oh, nothing. I just wanted you to watch the kids while we prayed."

I've thought this over for a good long time, say, ten years. Not constantly, just whenever the memory reared its ugly head. I would like to believe that the whole incident would have faded into obscurity if Tom had just asked me to watch the kids. Instead, I was left with high expectations that crashed into a million pieces. I had my annual cry that night, one that more than made up for the lack of tears on all the other nights.

Before I knew it, my annual crying bouts were giving way to more frequent sobfests. Randy had once commented that he believed many of the people he met in southern Delaware were suffering from a kind of "low-grade depression." If he was right, then maybe I had been living there long enough to acquire that condition for myself. Whatever I was suffering from, it was low-grade for sure.

My tendency to work too much didn't help matters. My resistance to prepackaged food kept me tied to the kitchen preparing all our meals from scratch. I sewed clothes for the kids and for myself. I crocheted and cross-stitched and quilted all kinds of things for our house. I even baked soy loaves for our dog so we wouldn't have to buy dog food. I was one step away from buying cows to milk and sheep to shear and wheat to grind and a horse for John to ride to work.

Instead of buying a standard curriculum program, I created my own customized home-schooling program some years. Other years, I used a curriculum that required massive amounts of teacher preparation and hands-on activities. And all the while, I continued to freelance, helping one woman write her memoir and writing articles for Christian and home-schooling magazines as well as several humor columns for a daily newspaper. It's no wonder I cried myself to sleep each night; I was too exhausted to pull my hair out.

On one of my many trips to the local library, I discovered a children's book called *Little Things*. To me, it's priceless — literally — because of the years of psychotherapy that this one book replaced. In it, an older woman named Mrs. B starts knitting a blanket; Mr. B is delighted, even though he has to wait for his supper. But little things like missing supper and breakfast the following morning never bother Mr. B. Gradually, Mrs. B's knitting project overtakes their lives, their house, and even their yard; still, it's such a little thing, and Mr. B remains unruffled. It's not until he has to search through mountains and mountains of knitted blanket to simply find his wife that he starts to come unglued. A surprised Mrs. B remarks that "little things" don't usually bother him. The ever-patient Mr. B gently points out that her blanket had become a very big thing.

Years of marital counseling could not have resulted in a more accurate depiction of our home life. Our small house was often overrun with schoolbooks, maps, charts, globes, half-finished sewing projects, the kids' craft projects—some waiting for the glue to dry, some on display—all adding up to Exhibit A, which I entered as evidence in the case I was making to prove my worth as a human being, wife, mother, and home-school teacher. And John just patiently took it, because little things never bothered him.

With all I had going on in my life, you'd think I would have had little time for introspection. But I couldn't escape the nagging feeling that there was still something missing, in both my private spiritual life and in our public worship. I had sensed it at the church in New Jersey, and I sensed it in Delaware. But I could not name it. Something in the pit of my spiritual being was empty and needed to be filled. Had I vocalized this to anyone in my church, I felt certain they would have offered up the usual charismatic answer to everything: "You need more of the Holy Spirit! Be filled, woman!" But that wasn't what I needed. Though I didn't know it at the time, it would take another interstate move and a series of physical crises to open my eyes to what was missing.

In the meantime, we had come to the conclusion that life in Delaware was not all that ideal. On the plus side, we had friends, church, home-schooling, and a new house on five wooded acres; on the minus side, John needed our only car to get to work, leaving the girls and me stranded out in the country, unable to get to a store or a friend's house or the library during the day. John often worked overtime at night and on weekends, which meant we didn't have transportation in the evenings or on weekends either. If we really, really needed the car, I could take John to work, but two round trips to Salisbury could take nearly three hours out of my day. The girls at times felt isolated and lonely, but buying a second car on one income was out of the question. We had been debt-free since leaving New Jersey, and we wanted to stay that way.

When John came home with the news that USAir was recruiting existing employees who were willing to be transferred to other cities, I was as attentive to him as I had ever been. One possibility was Charlotte, North Carolina. That sounded great to me; we had friends not far from there, two families who had escaped from the church in New Jersey around the time we had. The second choice, though, was the more likely one—Jacksonville, Florida. Florida? No way! I told John that never in a million years would I live in Florida, not with all the bad memories I had from my childhood trips there. Florida was where my mother's family lived, a place I associated with my enfeebled, emaciated, dying grandfather; a state that tolerated roaches as big as mice, attracted killer lightning on a regular basis, and held the original patent on the term *hot and humid*. That's where I went to get help and got seduced instead. That's where God had turned His back on me. No thanks—anywhere but Florida.

John didn't say much more about those transfer opportunities, and in time, I forgot about them. But I was itching to move again. Once again, our church—one of the main reasons we had moved to Delaware in the first place—was no longer enough to keep us there. I felt as if it had taken a massive crowbar to pry us loose from New Jersey, but now that we had been unwedged for so long, there was no limit to where we could go to live. Delaware had been a safe choice five years earlier, close enough to New Jersey so that we could go back every now and then if we wanted to. I was ready for something wild and risky, like moving to Alaska or Canada or any other place where the landscape was open and free and biting cold.

Which naturally meant that we would be moving to Florida.

CHAPTER 23

About the best thing that I can say for the Orlando area is that it isn't Miami. Flying into Orlando International Airport gives travelers the impression that the area is an inland paradise of pristine lakes and manicured lawns and plentiful trees. Outside the terminal, the landscape artists have strategically placed jasmine or honeysuckle or other perfume-laden flowers all around so their intoxicating fragrance will entice you into believing that this is, indeed, the Eden of the western hemisphere.

ତ⑨ ତ⑨ ତ⑨

AFTER YOU'VE LIVED THERE A WHILE, you realize that every lake is infested with alligators, that the maintenance of those manicured lawns costs a fortune in time and money, and that the trees you see from the air must be fake, some kind of deceptive overlay, because everywhere you look, the trees have been removed to make way for highways and parking lots and shopping malls and the seemingly impossible—even more housing developments.

There's this one huge lake, Lake Jesup, that I used to see every time I went to the airport, which was often. There were never any boats out on the lake, which I thought was really bizarre. *What's the matter with these people?* I would wonder. *Don't these people know what lakes are for?* I finally mentioned this to a neighbor, who told me about the alligators and the snakes and accumulated trash that prevented anyone with half a brain from going near Lake Jesup. I stored that information in at least half of my brain for safekeeping.

It turned out that it wasn't a job for John in Jacksonville that lured us to Florida. This move was all my fault. My freelancing had earned me a trip to a writers' conference in May 1993 in the Chicago area, where I was able to reconnect with Randy and his family for a day or so before the conference started. At the conference, I had a five-minute conversation with Lee Grady, who was then the news editor at *Charisma* magazine. He was looking for freelance reporters. I was looking to get away from news writing and try my hand at something else for a while, but what the heck. I handed him my résumé and writing samples and let it go at that.

Several months later, Lee called with an assignment for me. I turned the story in, didn't hear any complaints, and waited to see if I would get any more assignments from him. I did, but I also got something I never expected: a job offer. Lee was looking for an assistant news editor, and I seemed to fit the bill.

Well now, this was an interesting turn of events. I wasn't looking for a job; I had planned to home-school my daughters until they graduated from high school. For two months, our home group prayed for us as we weighed our options and considered the myriad ways this move would affect our lives. Meanwhile, the editorial department in Florida was praying as well.

John and I knew that a great opportunity had pretty much landed in our laps. If I was ever going to return to full-time employment, this was the way to do it. But it was in Florida. Florida! Why couldn't they publish the magazine in Colorado Springs or Carol Stream, Illinois, or Grand Rapids, Michigan, or any of the other areas of the country where Christian publishing houses were located? This was not going to be an easy decision.

In early March 1994, an ice storm hit southern Delaware with a vengeance. Six inches of ice coated everything in sight. Power poles snapped like Tinkertoys. Roofs collapsed; cars skidded off the roads and into icy ditches. Some areas lost power for a full week. The day after the storm, the sun began thawing the ice; that night, more ice formed, creating continued havoc.

Our driveway was crisscrossed with downed pine trees. Because I had this romantic image of a little house nestled among the pines, we had built our house within fifteen feet or so of the pine-filled woods. But the pines were much taller than that, so the girls and I huddled together in the house, listening to the snapping of one pine tree after another and wondering when one of those trees would come crashing through the roof. John spent three days just clearing trees from our 150-foot driveway.

That pretty much did it for me. I love cold weather and snow, but this ice storm was enough to drive a person mad. A month earlier, a very different ice threat had hit the area: Every road was suddenly covered with black ice, a layer of ice so thin that you can't see it. The girls and I had been at a friend's house, where it was raining and 50 degrees or so—practically balmy for February. By the time we left, the temperature had plummeted, and the roads were slick and treacherous. I could not drive faster than ten miles per hour without skidding; part of the way home, I followed a car that was moving forward but whose front wheels were turned at a forty-five-degree angle. It took us well over an hour to drive twelve miles.

Those two weather events, coming so close together, started to make Florida appear a bit less distasteful. I agreed to fly to Orlando for an interview. Maybe they wouldn't want me after all, and we wouldn't have to make this difficult decision. I talked myself into believing that I wouldn't have fit in anyway, so if they decided I wasn't right for the job, it would all be for the best.

But that's not the way it went. In the intervening months, the editor of *Charisma* had resigned, and Lee had been promoted to fill his position. They needed a news editor, not an assistant news editor. They decided I did fit in, and they offered me the job. John and I decided I should take it. *So what if I hate Florida? What if God had told me to go to the mission field in Somalia? I would go, right? That's* how my reasoning went, and that's how I perceived Florida, coequal with Somalia.

At ten, Elizabeth was less than thrilled with the news. Though she had not been particularly happy in Delaware, she was old enough to remember our move from New Jersey. She remembered what it was like to leave everything that was familiar to her—the neighborhood, her friends, her special places. Sarah, who had just turned six, was thrilled beyond measure. She imagined living in a house flanked by Disney World on one side and Universal Studios on the other.

With these great expectations in tow, our family moved from little Delaware to big and populous Florida. The culture shock was tangible; the traffic alone nearly did us in, especially after living in an area that had probably never experienced a true traffic jam. For the first year, my salary allowed John to play stay-at-home dad, driving Elizabeth back and forth to the private school we had enrolled her in. Sarah was able to start first grade in a school run by the company I was now working for, Strang Communications. That made the transition from home-schooling more bearable for her and for me. We could see each other throughout the day, and sometimes I would take her out for lunch.

Though the transition was difficult, that first year was made easier by the company and by my co-workers. People pitched in and did whatever they could to make us feel at home. John wasn't able to find a job right away, which was a bit surprising, but that didn't alarm me. It helped me to know that he was there for the girls while I was at work.

One thing I had been assured of before we made the decision to move was that we would have no trouble finding a church. There were so many in Central Florida, churches of all stripes and hues; Orlando was quickly becoming a mecca for Christian churches and organizations. Encouraged by those glowing reports,

I set out to find a church where our whole family would feel comfortable.

Starting with the churches that my co-workers attended, I visited a different church each Sunday—for months. I hadn't expected it to take that long. I assumed that by the second or third week, I would have found a suitable congregation. But just about everywhere I went, I found the same performance-driven atmosphere. Up front, the leaders were putting on a show for Jesus; in the pews—or folding chairs—the people were performing for the leaders, doing whatever the leaders wanted them to do. I might as well have been back in New Jersey.

And I got a crash course in the culture of Central Florida as well, like in the regional definition of *casual*. I missed the informal atmosphere of our church in Delaware, so I gravitated toward those churches that people described as casual, figuring I would fit right in. But no. *Casual* meant designer styles for golfing and yachting and cruising the Caribbean. More than once, I felt as if I had walked into a country club banquet hall rather than a church. In other churches, the dress was clearly Sunday best. It would be 95 degrees out with at least 100 percent humidity, and the men would be wearing suits and ties, the women suits and panty hose. This, I decided, was nuts.

I eventually found a church I liked, but the kids hated it; a few months later, we bought a house in an area so far from that church that it was no longer an option anyway.

What was going on here? I worked for a Christian company, in an area with a high Christian population, and I couldn't find a church to save my soul. For a year, we attended a church that wasn't a good fit, but it was nearby. One night, I took a chance and went to a service at a church affiliated with the Rhema Bible Training Center and Kenneth Hagin's ministry in Tulsa. This was a "word of faith" church, and honestly, I don't know whatever possessed me to give it a try. I had seen enough of the abuses of the positive-confession type of ministries; I wasn't about to willingly subject myself to any more of that kind of oppression.

But there I was, spiritually malnourished, wanting, hoping, praying that I would find a church before I died, so at least the pastor wouldn't have to give a generic eulogy: "And so today, we remember our dearly departed sister, _____, who was known to many but not to me." I went in, listened to a sermon that was actually about the Bible, and thought, *Not bad.* I went back, and I kept going back for three years. The pastoral couple, John and Jennifer Gryglewicz, proved to be two of the most down-to-earth, reasonable people I had ever met in ministry. I overlooked the whole Rhema "name it and claim it" thing.

And there were bikers in the church! Bikers! I fit right in. This church did not attract the country club set; it was about as culturally diverse a congregation as I had found anywhere in the area.

Finally, we were settled. We had bought a house, found a church, and got the girls settled in school. A year or so later, John also landed a job at Strang. On the surface, things were going great.

Except that deep down, I was thoroughly miserable. What on earth was wrong with me? I loved my family, my church, my job. I loved the people I worked with. I loved the company I worked for. I even loved going to Toronto on assignment every now and then to check out the Toronto Blessing, the "laughing revival" that had broken out in a church there. I laughed right along with them and thought I was free of all the baggage I had been carrying for so many years. What was going on?

To borrow another of my mother's Southernisms, it was time for the chickens to come home to roost.

I had never dealt with my horribly skewed relationship with God. I had not come to terms with some of the worst abuses I had suffered in New Jersey. I had never spent enough time alone with myself to know what I was about anymore or what was causing this severe emotional pain.

After a trip to Delaware over Christmas vacation in 1995, I started to unravel. I still hated Florida and hated myself for dragging my family there. I missed our friends and the remnants of our families up north. I even started to miss the northeast itself, with its dreary winters and hazy summers. I was coming unglued.

And this was the condition I was in as the March 1996 women's conference neared.

CHAPTER 24

From all indications, I didn't end my life that weekend at the Radisson. But I did get up from the floor, which took just about all my energy and willpower. I had neither the strength nor the desire to cry. I managed to leave my hotel room, and as a symbolic act representing my freedom from religion, I decided to do the most spiritual thing I could think of—go play with the dolphins at Sea World. But on the way to my car, I ran into a co-worker's spouse, a woman who was able to recognize the deadness in my eyes. Feeling drained and rejected herself, she suggested we go to her room to pray. I didn't have the heart to tell her my praying days were over, so I agreed. She prayed, she cried, and I called for room service. Forget feeding my spirit; it was my body that needed to be fed.

ဆဝ ဆဝ ဆဝ

I SHOULD HAVE REALIZED that I had hit rock bottom, but because I hadn't turned to anything to replace God, I guess I figured I wasn't there yet. I mean, I hadn't taken a drink or a snort of anything, nor did I want to. I wasn't tempted to do anything sinful or illegal. To anyone else, perhaps, an imaginary flat line across an imaginary hospital monitor might have provided a clue that a major part of me had died, but it meant nothing to me that day.

Back at work at the magazine the following week, it was life as usual, minus any expectations from God. Over the previous year, I had been working on a book with a woman named Sheryl who had battled severe depression; the book never came to pass, but a lasting friendship had developed. Meanwhile, Sheila Walsh, former cohost of *The 700 Club*, had written a book called *Honestly*, in which she described her battle with depression. I suggested we run a feature on depression highlighting Sheryl's story, along with a sidebar on Walsh, in an issue close to Christmas, a time when millions of people—many of them Christians—suffer from a seasonal bout with depression. Neither Walsh's nor Sheryl's depression was seasonal, but we hoped the timing would be helpful to believers who felt they had nowhere to turn when they sank into a pit of holiday despair. Depression was something that charismatics in particular had a difficult time admitting to.

I could have done the interview with Walsh by phone, but as luck, or God, would have it, she would be in Florida in April. We scheduled a lunch meeting, and on the way there—a three-hour ride for me—I planned to listen to the audio version of *Honestly*.

It's a good thing I left early—I always do; I'm so neurotic about being on time that to me *on time* means "late"—because twice during the drive, I had to pull over until I stopped crying. Had an alert state trooper been on the road that day, I'm sure she would have figured out a way to cite me for DUI—driving under the influence, not of alcohol but of tears. I should have been taken off the road.

Our lives were so different, but in Walsh's story, I heard echoes of my own. Like Walsh, I had lost the will to live; like her, I lived in the shadows, afraid to expose my true self for fear of even further rejection. In describing the darkest days of her battle, Walsh wrote: "I never knew God lived so close to the floor." That forced me off the road and onto the side, where I could rest my head on the steering wheel and cry all I liked, giving little thought to the narrowness of the shoulder on Florida's Turnpike or the proximity of the eighteen-wheelers whizzing by.

Ten minutes later, I pulled myself together as best I could, forced myself to stop crying so my eyes wouldn't be bloodshot when I met Sheila, and allowed the image of God living close to the floor to roam around in my mind for a while. Is it possible, I wondered, that

He had been with me on the floor at the Radisson, that He had not abandoned me but instead had been holding me all along?

No, I decided, that wasn't possible.

Ever the objective journalist, I met Sheila and proceeded to ask her all manner of questions about her depression in a most detached and professional way. OK, so maybe my eyes welled up a few times as we talked, but I hoped she would just surmise that I was a deeply compassionate sort of journalist. I didn't fool her, though. Several years later when I interviewed her for a Christian Web site, she told me she knew that I had been able to relate to her story on a much more personal level than I let on over lunch that day.

Back on the turnpike, the tears flowed pretty much nonstop. This was getting ridiculous, especially because pulling over on the shoulder was dangerous for another reason: There had been a rash of carjackings on highways throughout Central Florida, and drivers had been warned not to pull over unless they had a true emergency. To me, this was an emergency. I had finally admitted to myself that I was suffering from depression, and now I was threatened with being crushed by a mountain of shame. I was an editor at a Christian magazine; I had been a praying, Bible-reading, Scripture-memorizing Christian for twenty-five years; I had a wonderful husband and two wonderful kids; I hated myself; I lived in the shadows; I had lost the will to live.

Once I got home, I told no one what I had come to discover about myself. Not knowing what else to do, I called the hotline run by our medical insurance company, requested some general information on psychologists, and dutifully took down the names and phone numbers of several counselors, but that's all I did. The paralysis so common to clinical depression had already set in. I never made a single call.

At least, not to a counselor. Several weeks later, alone in my office at work, I found myself on the phone with my pastor. I'm assuming I called him, but I have no memory of making the call. My brain had disconnected once again, but this time it gave me fair warning: For an hour, maybe longer, I had sat at my desk, unable to think, unable to move, unable to function. Fast-forward, in slow motion, to me on the phone with my pastor. He asked me what was wrong. "Depression," I whispered, the first time I had ever uttered the word in connection with myself.

What he said next proved to be far more significant than he or I could imagine at that moment: "Have you seen a doctor? You need to get to a doctor right away." Here was a word of faith pastor urging me to get medical attention, just about the very last brand of pastoral leader that I would expect to give that kind of advice. No positive confession, no three-point biblical plan for dealing with despair, no "Three hallelujahs and call me in the morning." Just get to a doctor, and call me immediately afterward. I did.

I'm certain that my pastor, John Gryglewicz, had no idea how significant his advice was, mainly because I never told him. Once the medication kicked in a few weeks later, I was feeling so much better that I did not want to revisit the circumstances of that day. Of course, he knew the obvious—that seeing a doctor, getting a medical diagnosis of depression, and starting on Prozac or one of its cousins was the quickest route to genuine healing. Until the chemicals in my brain were functioning properly, he knew that I would not be able to heed any advice he gave me through the counseling that followed.

What he didn't know, and what I could not have articulated at the time, was that by urging me to get medical attention, he paved the way for a pivotal change in my relationship with God and the way I viewed Him. All of my life, way down deep inside my spirit, buried under piles and piles of doctrinal layering, misguided teaching, and self-induced overthinking, I knew that God had been ever present in my life. That mound of mess had not only obscured Him from my view but had also served as a convenient barrier protecting me from what He wanted to show me about my true self. It was easier at times to think He had abandoned me than to deal with the issues that made me keep Him at arm's length and beyond.

Pastor John snapped me out of the delusion that I could prescribe my own cure. By sending me to a doctor, he helped bring back to the surface of my life that deeply held conviction that God was everywhere, even in the doctor's office, even at the pharmacy, even as I swallowed my first antidepressant.

Years before, back in New Jersey, we had been taught that the solution to every problem and every ailment could be found in a variety of religious exercises: praying, reading the Bible, attending church, speaking in tongues, dancing in the Spirit, praising God in the Spirit, submitting to the leadership in the Spirit, becoming a Stepford wife in the Spirit. Until you have been paralyzed by depression, you cannot understand what a waste of time it is to tell a severely depressed person to practice even the worthwhile activities on that list. You might as well give the same advice to a person trapped under the rubble in a collapsed coal mine; he can't hear you, he can't move, and he's quickly running out of oxygen. You have to remove the rubble and pull him out of the suffocating darkness first. Only then can you work to mend the broken bones and stop the internal bleeding.

Zoloft, a cousin to Prozac, moved the mound of mess in my life and pulled me out of the suffocating darkness. Pastor John and Jennifer were now able to help me face the brokenness and allow God to repair the internal damage. They continued by prescribing the next step in their customized treatment program: They told me to get out and have some fun. Had I followed through on that bit of advice, my healing would have no doubt been accelerated. But I was committed and driven and intent on being the best editor I could possibly be. Fun, I thought, could wait.

The long-term healing may have been slow in getting off the ground, but for now, Zoloft enabled me to function as normally as I ever had. It bugs me when I hear people refer to antidepressants as "happy pills." They don't make you happy; they restore you to your normal self. Which in my case may not have been such a great thing, but you take what you can get.

I didn't exactly shout all this from the housetops, but I selectively began dropping clues about my battle to some of my co-workers. In the space of two months, a half-dozen women I worked with came to my office to talk to me. I always knew when a woman had come to talk about her depression, because she would either close the door or ask permission to close it. None had talked openly at work about the depression that had threatened to engulf her. All were either on antidepressants or had been. Most had not sought or received help from their church; all were afraid of losing their jobs. And each woman knew of other women in the company who were also suffering from depression.

It didn't take long for me to recognize the common threads that ran through our lives. Each of the women who came to see me felt as if she didn't fit in—not with her co-workers, not at her church, not even among her circle of friends. Each was an overworked per-fectionist; they were all simply going through the motions of life, having given up on any hope of an intimate, two-way relationship with God.

Nearly every one of them broke down and cried in my office.

Other than a listening ear and an empathetic hug, I had little to offer them. Had I realized how much I still had to sort out in my own life, I might have hung a "Do Not Disturb" sign on my office door. Had they realized how much I still had to sort out, they might have avoided me altogether. I was far from healed.

ରେ ରେ ରେ

ONE LOOK AT MY WORK DIARY over the next two years is enough to make a grown woman — me — break down and cry. Six months after I went on Zoloft, I was feeling great, well enough to take on the challenge of becoming managing editor of a Christian trade magazine published by the company I worked for.

The previous editor had worked long hours, around sixty hours a week. Well, I would change that. My newspaper experience had turned me into a fast worker, and I set out to implement streamlined, newspaperlike procedures for doing just about everything. But every time we started making headway, a new project would come along that quickly filled the gap and then some. In my eighteen months in that position, I worked exactly one forty-hour week, and that was only because I forced myself to do it, just so I could say that I had achieved such a stunning accomplishment. The previous week, of course, I had worked sixty-plus hours, the week after, seventy hours. I seldom took a real lunch break; most days, I ate at my desk. Every night and every weekend, I took work home with me.

The Gryglewiczes kept after me to stop working so much and go out and have the fun they had prescribed. But I couldn't see any way that I could possibly do that; the work kept piling up, and the staff was so small that there was no one to delegate the work to. I seldom took a full week's vacation. I would end up taking a few days off here and there, always carrying some of my vacation days over to the next year. Our family had never been big on annual vacations, so I didn't even have their griping to shake some sense into me.

My co-workers tried to warn me. Pastor John and Jennifer tried to warn me. Colleagues in the publishing industry tried to warn me. Former employees of the company tried to warn me.

And then one day, my heart tried to warn me.

I had long been accustomed to an erratic heartbeat. At times, my heart would take off on its own, on a kind of hundred-yard dash. It would race along at so fast a clip that it felt like a single stuttering ten-second beat. When it hit the finish line, it would resume its normal erratic rhythm, and I would go on with my life. But one day in October 1997, it pulled a real fast one on me. This one would be a marathon race.

It started out as a typical, abnormal racing. But it didn't stop—not after ten seconds, not after five minutes, not after fifteen minutes. Not wanting to alarm anyone, I called my doctor, whose office was five minutes away. Actually, describing this as a call to "my doctor" is comical; the practice had a high turnover in physicians as well as a rotating crop of physician's assistants, and you seldom saw the same person twice. In retrospect, I realized that I had placed my life in the hands of a bored, gum-cracking receptionist. I could come in if I wanted to, she told me, but there was no guarantee anyone would have time to see me. I did as she said, but by the time I got there, I was beginning to be truly alarmed. I explained my symptoms to the receptionist once again; she told me to have a seat.

As I was asking if I could possibly lie down somewhere, a doctor happened to walk through the receptionist's office. Somehow, she sensed that something was seriously wrong and asked me why I was there. I told her, and all heck broke loose. The doctor called 911, reprimanded the receptionist, got me to a gurney, and called my husband, all in the space of a few seconds. My heart had been racing at two hundred beats per minute for nearly an hour.

On the way to the hospital, the paramedics rebooted my system. No kidding. They gave me an injection that stopped my heart and then—praise the good Lord—restarted it. I can't say that it was one of the better experiences I ever had with drugs, but the paramedics did a good job of telling me what to expect before they did it. The sensation was eerie, to put it mildly.

That was pretty much it. I spent the requisite six hours being ignored in the emergency room. A cardiologist would wander in every now and then to take some readings, but basically I was on my own. Everything was normal, they said, and they sent me home with a referral to see a cardiologist. I did, and everything was normal. I found little comfort in that.

I took this as a distinct indication that my lifestyle needed an overhaul. I would start to take it easy, get some exercise, eat better, and have some fun. And still put out the magazine every three weeks or so. Right.

Seven months later, I returned for a repeat performance in the emergency room of the same hospital.

CHAPTER 25

After returning from my first scare in the emergency room, I was caught in a classic Catch-22 at work. As team leader on the magazine, I was responsible for handling problems that arose when there was a question or conflict between the advertising, editorial, and production departments. Usually, this involved money, but because I was not a director of the company, I did not have access to the weekly financial reports that contained the information I needed to handle the problem.

ᏸᏸ ᏸᏸ ᏸᏸ

ON NUMEROUS OCCASIONS, I brought this to the attention of the powers that be, but nothing ever changed. Members of the team would come to my office, challenge me about some item in the report, complain to me about some disparity in the report, and demand that I make the necessary changes before the next report came out. But I wasn't allowed to see the report.

This was not the kind of fun Pastor John had recommended. And this was not the way to treat a perfectionist. I tried to develop a workaround, a way to solve problems without the basic information I needed to solve the problems. Not surprisingly, it didn't work.

Attending church was pretty much impossible. Between work and work-related travel, I had attended a service or two in April and May 1998. The first Wednesday in June, I made up my mind that I was going to attend that evening's midweek service. I did not take any work home that night, although I knew I was treading on thin ice. The magazine's annual advisory board dinner meeting was a month away, and I had neither reserved a room for the dinner nor made any plans for the meeting itself. That's the kind of task I never had time for during the day, when simply getting the magazine out the door required all of my attention.

As I drove to church that night, my body was shaking from fatigue. Once I arrived, several people tried to talk to me, but my mouth could not form any words by way of response. I ducked into the sanctuary—OK, the all-purpose room—found a seat, and tried to stop shaking. I needed sleep. I needed peaceful sleep. I needed long peaceful sleep. If I hadn't been so exhausted, I would have gotten up and left. I was too tired to move.

That night, in response to a challenge from the speaker, I gave it all up to God—mainly my job, but everything else in my life. Not that there was all that much, of course, but somehow I had managed to keep my husband and kids from leaving me, which I can only attribute to the grace of God and John's extraordinary gifts as a husband and father. My relationship with God was as complicated as ever, but desperate times call for desperate action. So maybe I hadn't been to church in ages, and maybe the only time I had opened my Bible in the last two months was to check a Scripture reference in an article I was editing. I had no choice; I had to take a chance that He would hear and respond. I told Him flat out, "God, I don't care anymore what You do. I want out. I can't take this job anymore, but I can't just walk out. Do something, anything, whatever it takes. I need relief."

He did something, all right. Twelve hours later, sitting in my office, my eyes started to vacillate. Whenever I try to describe this condition, people think I mean a simple eye tic, where your eyelids or the skin around your eyes get this little nerve twitch. That is not what happened, believe me. I mean my eyeballs started to vacillate; I could hear them vacillating inside my head. And I thought that rebooting in the ambulance was a weird sensation! This was spooky, and it wouldn't stop. I couldn't walk, because I couldn't keep my balance. I couldn't drive. A friend drove me to the doctor, who prescribed bed rest.

The next morning, I was worse off than ever. Once John left for work, the only way I could get anything I needed was to crawl.

I called the health plan hotline once again. The nurse told me to hang up and call 911 immediately; based on the way I described my symptoms to her, there was a real possibility that I was having a stroke. Once I got to the emergency room, the long wait started again. In the meantime, John had arrived. We looked at each other—well, I looked at him as well as I could, given my vision problem—and we both knew: It was over. I could not and would not return to the job I had.

Over the next two months, I had to learn to live with my unsettling condition. The emergency room doctor told me he had come across my condition only once before, and that case had cleared up within an hour or two. An MRI showed no organic problems. Countless trips to a neurologist—who later thanked my doctor for referring to him "this most interesting patient"—revealed nothing conclusive. The official diagnosis, and a halfhearted one it was, indicated that I was suffering from chronic anxiety brought on by persistent, relentless stress. Well, shoot, I knew that much, at least the part about the stress. I wouldn't have characterized my emotional state at the time as anxious, but one thing I've since learned is that a person suffering from chronic anxiety doesn't necessarily feel anxious.

The only thing that stopped my eyes from vacillating was another antidepressant called Effexor, but we didn't discover that until I had tried numerous other medications. Effexor was a long shot, but it worked. It's been four years since I started taking it, and even now, if I forget a dose, my eyes start right back up again. There appears to be no cure for my condition. Effexor only relieves the symptoms.

For four months after my trip to the emergency room, I continued to do my regular job from home, with the staff back in the office taking up the slack. I was bedridden for three of those four months. It wasn't until the fourth month that I could walk to the mailbox down the road.

Finally, though, I was in nearly constant communication with God. I had come to depend on Him for just about everything except room service, which my family provided. I had a million questions, too: How could I leave my job? I had made a commitment to the company, and once I make a commitment, I follow through with it. The Lord gently reminded me that my commitment to Him and to my family took precedence over my commitment to the company. He and my family had gotten short shrift for years, and then there was the rather obvious matter of my health.

And there, confined to my bed for so many weeks, I faced the truth about my life. I loved God; I hated church. I loved my family; I hated the little time I had for them. I loved writing and editing; I hated what my job had become.

Admitting that I hated church wasn't all that hard. I had even told Jennifer, my pastor's wife, that church drove me crazy. The problem, which I would not recognize for another few years, was my narrow conception of church. Not the church as a living organism, which I had long ago understood to be a united body of believers transcending religious denominations and buildings and organizations and institutions. The problem came when I thought of *going* to church, to a particular building or assembled congregation. At that time, the only image that came to mind was that of an independent charismatic or evangelical church.

My daughters, now eleven and fifteen, had other ideas. They felt they did not fit in with the kids at the church that the Gryglewiczes pastored. I listened to their concerns for several weeks, recognized the misfit pattern that they had obviously inherited from John and me, and reluctantly agreed to switch to a denominational church whose youth group was a better fit for them. It was OK, but I soon stopped going to church altogether. No matter where I went—and I did try numerous other churches—the service seemed like a performance, especially where the worship team was concerned. All too often, a worship leader would take off on his or her own interpretation of a praise song, leaving the congregation stranded and mute.

And of course, people still looked at me funny—not only at church, but everywhere I went. Complete strangers would gape at me as if to say, "Don't you know there's something wrong with you?" Well, yes. I'm just not sure what.

Once, when I was alone on a trip out west to visit a friend, I decided to grab a take-out order from an Olive Garden restaurant to eat in my hotel room. The bartender, doubling as waiter for take-out customers, asked what I'd like. "Cappellini pomodoro and a salad with house dressing, please." That's all I said. Really.

He stopped writing on his order pad, gave me this penetrating, concerned look, and asked, "Are you all right?"

Well, no, I thought, *but how did you know?* Instead of being sarcastic, I groused about the long flights that day, all the delays, how I was as tired as all get out.

He stared at me a few seconds longer and finished writing the order. I asked for a Diet Coke while I was waiting. He asked, "Are you sure you're all right?" I tried to assure him that I was, but even as he tended to his other customers, he kept a wary eye on me. What was he afraid of? That I would keel over? Go postal? Skip out on the bill? I have no idea. I paid for my order, picked up the bag, and headed for the door, knowing his eyes were on me the whole time.

It's nuts, absolutely nuts. Just when I start to think that my misfittedness is all in my head, some punk bartender blows that illusion to bits. If it hadn't been him, then it would have been the cashier at the supermarket who stopped three times and stared at me while ringing up my under-ten-item order. I checked my teeth for spinach as soon as I got out to the car. Nothing in my teeth, nothing in my hair, nothing on my shirt. Nothing. Just me and my royal weirdness, I suppose.

I tried not to let other people bother me. I had more important things to think about. There was still something missing, something I couldn't pinpoint. I needed to figure out what it was.

CHAPTER 26

One of the missing pieces in the church puzzle was obvious. No matter what church I attended, true worship of God seemed to be missing or at least lacking. That was only part of the problem; besides, I wasn't all that certain that I knew what true worship looked like. I only knew what it didn't look like. And I don't mean to imply that I thought the people in all those churches were not worshiping God; there was something missing for me and maybe me alone.

☙ ☙ ☙

BECAUSE I HAD NEVER BEEN a typical church-hopper—that horrendous category of believer, worse than an infidel, worse than a hypocrite—this church search was really starting to get to me. *Church-hoppers,* people who flitted from one congregation to another as soon as they found something about a church that they didn't like, were routinely blasted from the pulpit. I tried to avoid getting a reputation for that, but no matter where I went, I couldn't shake the feeling that I was playing church. Every time I thought I had found a church that was different, I would hold my breath, keep my hopes in check, and give it a try. I usually didn't have to wait long before I exhaled and exited.

On a business trip to a rodeo—not as strange as it sounds: I was there to do a story on rodeo ministries—I attended a small service conducted by a low-key itinerant cowboy ministry. Afterward, the person who invited me to the service introduced me to one of the pastors. As I stood there talking to him, I was jarred by the awareness that he never took his eyes off me. He never looked around for someone more important to talk to. He looked me straight in the eye and listened to every word I said. As we shook hands and turned away from each other, tears began to well up in my eyes. He had listened to me. He wanted to hear what was in my heart. He didn't look over my head to find a more influential person to greet. He gave me hope that maybe, just maybe, I fit in.

I was ready to move out west and join a cowboy church, just like that. Meeting in a barn with hay-bale pews and horse manure on the ground suddenly sounded heavenly.

Once I was back home again, I gave up on church. I knew I would return someday, but I wasn't up for the search. Meanwhile, an old familiar desire tugged at me. I wanted to go to a monastery. Not join one, just visit one for a day or a week or a month. And I would not be trying to escape from my problems; if anything, I figured I would be facing them head on. Unlike one of my pastors, who slammed monks for trying to hide from the world, I figured the monastic life was just about as hard as it gets. I never joined a commune in the 1960s, partly because no one wanted me, but even if an invitation had been extended, I would have declined, knowing how hard it is to live with other people. How a community of monks can stand being with each other day in and day out is beyond me. In a marriage, at least you get to choose your housemate. Monks have no such luxury. A monastery is not a place for the faint of heart.

Thumbing through a guide to monasteries that I'd borrowed from the library, I discovered a few within a reasonable driving distance that sounded good. I started to wonder if I would fit in, but I dismissed that concern right away. Monks aren't known for being normal, and from what I understood, they pretty much had to take you in, hospitality being right up there with poverty, chastity, and obedience. I would appear at the door, and no matter which monk greeted me, he would have to welcome me and resist the urge to look at me funny.

I mentioned all this to an editor, who suggested I try out an ecumenical prayer center in southern Georgia that conducted silent personal retreats. Well now, that sounded different. A silent retreat? That certainly appealed to me, but I wasn't sure it would cure what ailed me. What I needed, I thought, was intense personal counseling to help me get at the root of my misfittedness, which had left me isolated, lonely, and churchless. When I discovered that the center offered spiritual direction—which I had craved after reading Susan Howatch's series of novels on the Church of England during the time I was confined to bed—I made the decision to go. Spiritual direction, a specific type of pastoral guidance that helps a person sort out her relationship to God and live out that relationship, sounded like just what I needed.

Before I left, my friend Angie, who had worked with me at Strang, suggested that we make another stab at finding a church. Her misfit nature had also isolated her from church; like me, she was tired of the emphasis on performance and the lack of focus on true worship. She wanted us to try out an Episcopal church nearby.

That's it, I thought. We've hit rock bottom. We're so desperate that she's suggesting we attend a liturgical church, a denominational church, and a liberal one at that. My impression of the Episcopal Church was that there were two camps, the liberal and the charismatic. I was somewhat disenchanted with the charismatic movement, and the church she named was definitely not charismatic. That meant it had to be liberal. Church Search 2002 was certainly getting complicated.

With some relief, I headed for southern Georgia, thankful that I could put off this Episcopal decision for two more Sundays. Six hours later, I arrived at the ecumenical prayer center, which turned out to be affiliated with the Episcopal Church. I must have missed those descriptions of the prayer center as I was making the decision to go there. As I had long known, God does have a sense of humor, and He's not afraid to use it.

By the end of my stay, I could hardly contain my own laughter. In those days of silence and solitude, I did indeed find a cure for loneliness. By going away by myself, with only God and my own thoughts for companionship, I discovered a rich, two-pronged relationship that far surpassed the social interaction that so often ended up making me feel even more lonely. One aspect of that relationship was with God, but the other part was with me. I found the courage to look at myself and listen to my thoughts and hear the cry of my own heart. I spent many of my quiet hours journaling and peeling off layer upon layer of "churchianity" that had hindered my fellowship with God. God was indeed good, and I wasn't half bad myself.

I marveled at how readily we retreatants were able to bond by wordlessly communicating with each other, through a hug or a smile or just a glance; I realized just how unnecessary small talk can be. Our days consisted of private time in the morning and, after our communal lunch, time to pray or walk or journal or read or just be. Daily Eucharist preceded a communal supper, followed by a brief evening prayer service. We lived intentionally, a concept I was just beginning to grasp. It was quite an experience for me to sit at a table with eight people and share a meal without speaking to each other, and not because we were ticked off. Every afternoon, we served each other the bread and the wine. I obediently avoided sipping the wine, honoring my vow to God to refrain from alcohol, but even so, I had never experienced such a profound and meaningful time of communion.

And through the spiritual direction I received, I rediscovered my longing for reflection and contemplative prayer. Both would become an integral part of my life, now that I had learned how to assimilate those practices into my very ordinary lifestyle.

᏶᠑ ᏶᠑ ᏶᠑

THE SUNDAY AFTER I RETURNED HOME, I agreed to attend the Episcopal church with Angie, but I can't say I had high hopes that this
would work out. After all, it was still a church, and not at all like this
intimate prayer center that I had come to love. But the prayer center
had opened my eyes to true God-centered worship, and I figured I
could apply what I had experienced there to a traditional church
service.

The only expectations I took with me to church that Sunday
were that everyone would look at me funny; no one except the official greeters would speak to me; and I would feel lost and out of
place when it came to the liturgy. All that was fine, I decided, as
long as I kept my focus on God.

So much for those expectations. No one looked at me funny; several people spoke to me as if I had been there forever; and I fell in
love with the liturgy. In fact, I fell in love with the Episcopal
Church. I turned to Angie and said, "I feel as if I've found my spiritual home. They speak a language I understand." I immediately
understood the deep and rich meaning of the rituals; I saw the
gospel in everything they did and said throughout the service; and I
rediscovered the awesome presence of a holy God in a church, of all
places. In fact, the centrality of Jesus stunned me. Everything, *everything*, pointed to Him—not to the rector, not to the sermon, not to
the music, but to Jesus. This was clearly an evangelical church.

I had found the missing spiritual link. It was the liturgy of the
Episcopal Church. No wonder my search had been so frustrating. I
had been looking in all the wrong places.

That first Sunday, I spent the rest of the day keeping the Sabbath
for the first time in years, but not in a legalistic sense. I wanted to
rest in the presence of God for the remainder of the day. The
remainder of my life, really, but again, you take what you can get.

The following day, I e-mailed my older brother, Bill, about something completely unrelated to my spiritual life. My timing was uncanny. He had just completed some genealogical research on our mother's family. The big news to him was that we were descended from an extremely wealthy family, but our great-grandmother had disowned our grandmother after she married a carpenter below her station. That would have been my Grandpa Schwall, the man on the stained mattress in the two-room clapboard house in Gainesville. For him, my grandmother lost a fortune.

But the big news for me was what Bill told me almost as an afterthought: He had traced our lineage back to a vicar in the Church of England in the 1600s. We came from a long line of Anglicans. The Episcopalians did indeed speak a language I understood; I had Anglican blood coursing through my veins to prove it.

Our Anglican ancestors had come to this country and eventually become Baptists. They started not only a Baptist church but also an entire town—forty-five minutes from the prayer center in southern Georgia. My ancestors had lived all throughout that area.

Had I truly found my place in the family of God? You bet I had. Not just in the Episcopal Church, not just in a specific prayer center in a specific time and place, but in a rich spiritual heritage that I was only beginning to discover and in a rich spiritual history that I had never appreciated. God had indeed been with me all along, even on the carpet at the Radisson, and He had indeed been showing me where I belong—with Him, whether I sense His presence or not.

CHAPTER 27

One of the most common birds in the western hemisphere is also one of the least familiar. It's called the sora rail, and when it can be found—which is not very often—it will most likely be spied among cattails and bulrushes and the ubiquitous muck of the marshlands. Soras can remain underwater for a surprisingly long time, poking their heads up every now and then to check out the lay of the land. But mainly, they lurk in the wetlands undergrowth, maintaining such a low profile that you're unlikely to spot one unless you—or your hound dogs—have the great fortune of flushing one out as you tramp through thick and wet vegetation. Even then, you'll only catch a quick glimpse of the sora skimming the tips of the grasses before it drops from flight in midair.

☙☙☙☙☙

SOMEHOW, THOUGH, THIS BIRD GETS AROUND, migrating two thousand miles to its wintering sites along the Gulf of Mexico and similar warm-climate habitats. The thing is, no one is really sure how it gets there from its summer habitats in places like Canada and Maine and Wyoming. Some ornithologists insist that it flies there, though no one has ever produced hard evidence of that, and *Wyoming Wildlife*—my chosen authority on this and a host of other wildlife matters—remains skeptical. How can a bird that generally restricts its movement to walking and gliding a few feet at a time—a "pathetic excuse for flight"—fly such an incredible distance as its migration patterns indicate? But then again, short of hitching a ride on a cruise ship, how else can the sora turn up on islands like Trinidad and the Bahamas?

It's one of the mysteries of the natural world, and it's one that *Wyoming Wildlife* editor Chris Madson attributes to the power of persistence, the persistence to get from point A to point B against all odds. And that's why now, if anyone should ever again ask me which animal I most identify with, I finally have an answer. In many respects, I am the human counterpart of the sora rail.

No doubt about it, the similarities are striking. Common and yet unfamiliar, I've lived in the muck and stayed down longer than seemed humanly possible. I've fought like crazy at times to keep a low profile, but someone—and we all know who He is—always managed to flush me out of my hiding places. But seldom for long. I'd retreat to the nearest and safest haven at the first opportunity.

I'm most like the sora rail, though, when it comes to our mutual migration patterns. As with the sora, no one can adequately explain how I got where I am today from where I started out. I can identify the landmarks along the way, and I can see how making a certain turn in my life led to all these other turns that brought me to my current resting place. But I can't see the big picture, partly because it isn't completed, of course, but also because that perspective is reserved for the One who set me on my migratory course in the first place. Now, I'm no ornithologist, but I suspect that a bird migrates in much the same way, from one landmark to another, living as it does without the benefit of a globe to give it perspective on the course of its entire flight.

And then there's the power of persistence, which I'm certain I inherited from a woman who got her driver's license when she was forty-seven and earned her G.E.D. when she was sixty and drove halfway across the country—and back again—by herself when she was seventy, without once getting lost or mugged or killed, simply to look up a grade-school friend. She persevered through more heartache and disappointment and abuse than any one person should ever have to handle, much of it from me. But my mother, God bless her, passed along to me the tenacity to keep holding on, even when my grip began to weaken and the rope looked mighty short.

But most of all, it was the power of God's merciful persistence that brought me safely from where I started to where I am. As in Francis Thompson's "Hound of Heaven," He dogged me with such persistence that I cannot help but recognize His distinctive tracks in my life. They're all over the map.

He was there, of course, when I turned to Him for His saving grace after I had made such a wretched mess of my life. He was there when I was—finally!—baptized, and when I first experienced the joy of leading someone else to Him, and as I watched Him work in the lives of the children and young people and women I felt responsible for, and as He forced me out of my hiding places and into visible ministry.

But never was God more fully present in my life than He was in those times when He seemed the farthest away. I know that now. His hand was the one that held back the waters that threatened to engulf me time and time again. His Spirit was the One who turned my thoughts back to the family I loved in this life when I wanted to chuck it all and go on to the next life. His people were the ones who formed a tight circle around me and kept me from crumbling when depression threatened to destroy me. And His Son was the One who steered me back to the profound reality of the cross whenever I allowed church to get in the way. He was most active in my life during those long and dry spells when I was sure He had given up on me completely, when I was convinced He was biding His time until I became the oldest living person on the planet. Only then would He deal with me and my inevitable demise.

Now whenever God seems far away, I can smile and enjoy yet another paradox of my life with Him, because I know He's nearer than ever. Like Sheila Walsh, I've discovered just how close to the floor God lives. I'm grateful for the gift of depression, which no longer has the power to terrorize me. I get a kick out of finding the cure for loneliness in solitude. I chuckle inside when people treat me like a misfit. These days, I'm downright amused when church folks seem to go out of their way to ignore me. And I've got to admit that it's pretty funny that I've finally found freedom of worship in the structure of a traditional liturgy.

ᘛᘚ ᘛᘚ ᘛᘚ

IT SEEMS TOO SIMPLE TO SAY this today: My place in the family of God is wherever God is. But there was nothing simple about the process that brought me to that discovery. And it's a deceptively simple statement, because churches have been arguing about where God is for millennia. Though I know that this side of heaven I'll probably never lose my habit of overthinking, I politely decline to get caught up in complex theological arguments anymore. Don't ask me where He is. My brain will no doubt skip a succession of beats, my eyes will glaze over, and by the time my brain kicks back in again, I will have formed an answer that bears no relation whatsoever to your original question, a response as disconnected as "Of course not."

And while I've found my congregational place in a liturgical church, I know that I will never discount the rich and varied personal history of church experience that God favored me with. From the Methodists, I first heard the gospel, the incredible story that I trust I will never tire of hearing. The Baptists and other evangelicals gave me a solid grounding in the Bible and in evangelism, and an unshakable respect for doctrinal truth and biblical scholarship. Roman Catholics introduced me to the charismatic renewal and to the hope that a contemplative life could be achieved even in America in the tumultuous 1970s. Independent charismatic churches and denominational Pentecostals expanded my spiritual life, restoring to me the joy of my salvation and giving me a host of reasons to laugh right out loud. Finally, the Episcopalians helped me rein all that in to a structure that resonates with me, in a liturgical language that I understand.

And although my spiritual home is now a liturgical church, I'm just as comfortable worshiping in an evangelical or a charismatic or a mainline church. It no longer matters whether or not I feel as if I belong among a particular congregation of people, because I've rediscovered the focus that for so long was missing from my church experiences, the focus on God Himself. When I travel, I'd be most likely to seek out an Episcopal church, but I'd have no problem worshiping with the Baptists or the Methodists or the Roman Catholics.

If push came to shove, I might even attend a service at a King James–only church. But I can't promise I won't be toting a pulpit-sized edition of *The Living Bible*, if such an edition exists. Then again, I've always given people a reason to look at me funny. Why stop now?

About the Author

MARCIA FORD IS A FORMER RELIGION EDITOR for the *Asbury Park Press* in New Jersey, associate editor of *Charisma* magazine, and editor of *Christian Retailing*. In 1999 she launched her own successful writing and editing business, Ford Editorial Services, and since 2001 has also been affiliated with WordSpring Media. The author of *Meditations for Misfits* and *Charisma Reports: The Brownsville Revival* and coauthor of *Restless Pilgrim: The Spiritual Journey of Bob Dylan*, she has written seven additional published books.

Marcia and her husband, John, live in Central Florida with their daughter Sarah. Their adult daughter, Elizabeth, lives nearby.

Marcia would love to hear from other misfits. You may contact her at Misfit@marciaford.com/

Meditations for Misfits:
Finding Your Place in the
Family of God
Marcia Ford
$12.95 Hardcover
ISBN: 0–7879–6400–X

Those of us who sometimes feel that we don't "belong" desire to find and understand the special place God has for us in His family. Misfits sometimes experience rejection and loneliness, which can also lead to depression and other emotional and spiritual disorders. But we all need to be reminded from time to time that God cares—and that Jesus Himself was viewed as a "misfit" in His day.

Meditations for Misfits is a humorous and wise collection of reflections designed to help self-perceived misfits experience reconciliation with God, with other people, and with themselves. Each of the weekly meditations uses Scripture, a quote or excerpt, and a prayer to underscore the intrinsic value of misfits and their special place in the family of God.

MARCIA FORD is a writer, principal in WordSpring Media, and contributor to Publishers Weekly Religion BookLine. She has been an editor for *Charisma, Christian Retailing, Ministries Today,* and iBelieve.com. She resides near Orlando, Florida, with her husband and children.

[Price subject to change]

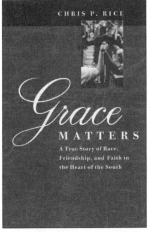

Grace Matters:
A True Story of Race, Friendship,
and Faith in the Heart of the South
Chris P. Rice
$22.95 Hardcover
ISBN: 0–7879–5704–6

Grace is the most potent counterforce at work in our violent species, and our only hope. Chris Rice gives a very personal account, at once inspiring and disturbing, of its transforming power.
—Philip Yancey, author, *What's So Amazing About Grace?*, *Soul Survivor*, and *Where Is God When It Hurts?*

Americans feel fatigued by racial divisions yet yearn to resolve them, to somehow live together in greater harmony and understanding. We all want a powerful, true story of success and hope, showing us that true racial reconciliation is indeed possible. This book tells that story. Imbued with the passion of his Christian faith, white college student Chris Rice left his studies at Middlebury College in Vermont to join the Voice of Calvary ministry in a tough urban neighborhood in Jackson, Mississippi. There he met Spencer Perkins, eldest son of John Perkins, legendary African American evangelist and civil rights movement activist.

In *Grace Matters*, Chris tells the story of this remarkable interracial faith community where he and Spencer and a dedicated group of black and white Christians worked together to realize the vision of the Sermon on the Mount and in so doing improve the impoverished lives of people in their neighborhood. At Antioch, as they called the community they founded, several families pooled all their resources and lives and set out on a journey to racial reconciliation and fidelity to their faith and its power.

For all those who wonder whether true racial reconciliation is possible, in this moving, powerful book Chris Rice shows that it is—but only with the help of God's grace and the dedication of those who seek the personal breakthroughs that can only be achieved by not giving up on each other, no matter what.

CHRIS P. RICE is currently pursuing studies at the Divinity School at Duke University. He is the winner of a Critic's Choice Award from *Christianity Today* magazine for his book *More Than Equals: Racial Healing for the Sake of the Gospel*, which he coauthored with Spencer Perkins. He has been a research associate for the Boston University Institute on Race and Social Division, a columnist for *Sojourners* magazine, and has written, spoken, and taught extensively on the subject of racial reconciliation.
[Price subject to change]